A Glossary:
Artificial vs.
Intelligent

SilvanaEditoriale

Northwestern | QATAR
media majlis museum

This book is published on the occasion of the exhibition
<u>Ai or Nay? Artificial vs. Intelligent</u>
on view at the Media Majlis Museum
at Northwestern University in Qatar
from 15 January to 15 May, 2025

Editors
Jack Thomas Taylor & Katy Gillett

Project Management
Katy Gillett

Illustrations
© Bilge Emir

Media Majlis Museum
Northwestern Qatar, a member of Qatar Foundation
Education City
Doha, Qatar
mediamajlis.northwestern.edu

In October 2022, the Media Majlis Museum at Northwestern University in Qatar received accreditation by the American Alliance of Museums (AAM). This achievement signifies the museum's quality and credibility to the museum community, to governments and outside agencies, and to the museum-going public. The Media Majlis is the first museum outside of the Americas to receive this accreditation.

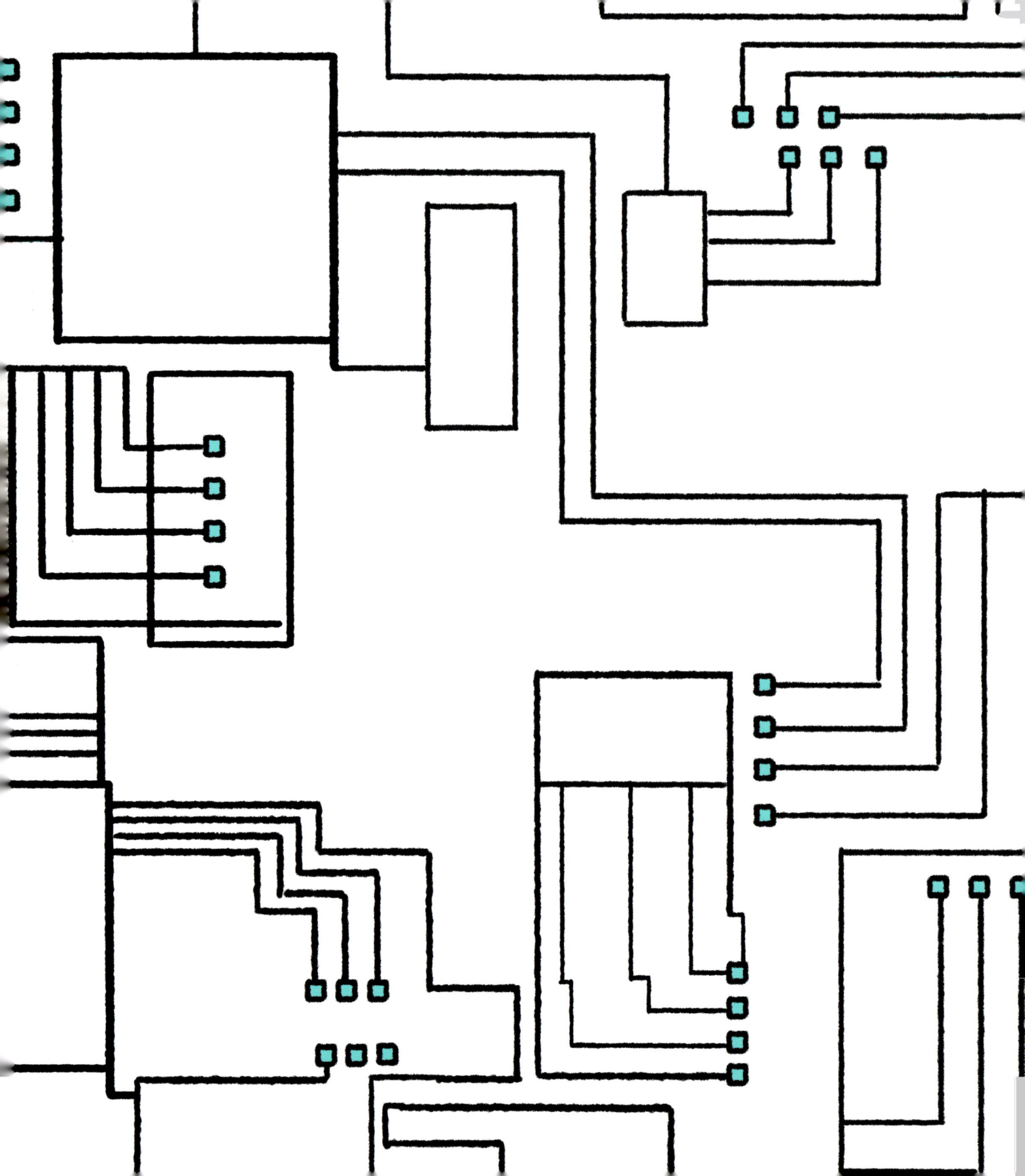

Contents

Foreword: Artificial vs. Intelligent

By Marwan M. Kraidy

I recently saw a cartoon that aptly captures the general feeling about artificial intelligence (AI). In a conversation between two adults, one says to the other something like: 'I am so excited about all the time that AI is going to free up for me ... so that I have more time to worry about the implications of AI.'

AI ambivalence is real for anyone whose thinking ventures beyond the easy dichotomy between an AI utopia—where smart learning machines drive themselves, develop cures for cancer and catalyze new discoveries that transform human lives—or an AI dystopia—where algorithmic overlords reign over human life through disturbing identitarian and class biases during peace and through terrifying killing machines in wartime.

In academia, narratives about AI tend to oscillate between doomsday 'the robots will take over' scenarios on the one hand, and dismissive 'nothing is new under the sun' perspectives on the other. Variants include doom and gloom about the deep challenges generative AI poses to academic integrity in the classroom and for writers and media makers; glib contrarianism that there is nothing to be concerned about; and uncritical celebration of AI's potential contributions to teaching, research and academic operations, without paying heed to its hazards.

Last year, we launched the Artificial Intelligence Initiative (AI²) as a new strategic enterprise at Northwestern University in Qatar (NU-Q). We at NU-Q uniquely contribute to humanity's understanding of AI, as we harness aspects of this technology's immense potential for humankind that are relevant to our mission, and develop and deploy critical research, teaching and professional tools. We want to confront what a recent Interim Report by the United Nations' AI Advisory Body, titled Governing AI for Humanity, called AI's 'known, unknown, and as yet unknowable harms.' From deepfakes to misinformation, chief concerns about AI are core to our media- and journalism-focused mission. With the wealth of AI-relevant expertise at NU-Q, we are ready to take up this challenge.

As a unique space of critical exploration at the intersection of art, media and technology, our Media Majlis Museum is a distinctive unit within our institution. With this new exhibit, Ai or Nay? Artificial vs. Intelligent, The Media Majlis Museum contributes to our understanding of AI and its impact on the issues that matter most to a media school with programs in communication, journalism and strategic communication, and liberal arts. Truth and falsehood, beauty and ugliness, knowledge and bigotry, are binaries of judgment that AI is poised to reshape. How journalists authenticate information, how artists create and provoke, and how researchers gather, analyze and interpret data, can all be harmed or boosted by AI.

Our job is to make sure we reap the benefits of AI without enduring its harms. Our aesthetic judgments inform our ethical predispositions and the worldviews that frame our professional and personal engagements. With its formidable exhibits, the Media Majlis Museum has compelled the community to be critical of clichés, bandwagons and received wisdoms. Most importantly, when we contemplate a haunting work of art, and as a result feel deeply and think more freely, visiting exhibits teaches us how to be better critics of ourselves.

It is with this spirit that I invite you to read this book, visit the exhibit and contribute to the ongoing conversation. I do so with great confidence in our ability to contribute meaningfully to the pressing questions that AI raises, in synergy with Northwestern's presidential priority to "harness the power of data analytics and artificial intelligence" (see ai.northwestern.edu), and in collaboration with Qatar Foundation's emphasis on AI as a priority area for Education City.

Our approach to AI does not arise in a vacuum. It is embedded within our institutional priorities and core values. It is grounded in Northwestern's commitments to excellence as one of the world's leading research universities. These also include "to foster interdisciplinary innovation between the social sciences and global studies"—something we at NU-Q excel at—and "to enhance the creative and performing arts," which our creative writers, filmmakers, digital game designers and artists do every day with gusto.

Consider this Media Majlis Museum exhibit as a culmination of the above. It will help give us the capacity, confidence and wherewithal to navigate the unchartered waters of the rapid and unpredictable developments in AI. It also positions NU-Q as a central player in shaping our understanding and application of AI in global higher education, and the media and creative industries worldwide.

Happy viewing.

Marwan M. Kraidy

Introduction: They don't know. We don't know.

By Jack Thomas Taylor

Introduction

As I delve into the development of an exhibition exploring AI, I find myself grappling with the challenge of explaining exactly what AI is. It seems to be everywhere, permeating our daily lives and conversations. The buzz is inescapable. Dozens of books are being published, whitepapers and trend reports flood inboxes, and conferences and symposiums occur on what feels like a weekly basis. Social media is saturated with grand statements proclaiming AI's potential to change the world and rhetorical questions pondering how it will transform everything we know. But is it worthy of all the attention it's garnering, and should we really be as concerned about it as many of us seem to be? Amidst this fervor, a straightforward question remains unanswered: What is AI? The truth is, no one can provide a definitive answer. Why? Because they don't know. We don't know. I don't know.

The study of AI has been ongoing since the 1950s[1], characterized by recurring phases of high enthusiasm and subsequent disappointments referred to as 'AI winters' and 'AI summers.' With each new method or strategy that arises, there is a surge in excitement followed by inevitable disillusionment, leading to another period of reduced interest. At present, we find ourselves in the midst of an AI summer, particularly within the field of generative AI.

Throughout human existence, we have been captivated by the idea of having an 'other' perform arduous labor on our behalf.[2] Whether it is through legendary stories of mythical beings protecting humans, religious beliefs in spiritual guardians or the ongoing presence of modern-day slavery, humanity has consistently found ways to exploit others, including fellow humans and animals as well as now machines. This raises unsettling questions: Are we on the brink of history repeating itself? What are the implications of our contemporary relationship with operating systems and machines? The historical context of AI and its parallels with slavery raise important questions about the power dynamics and ethical implications of these technologies.

Insight

The origins of AI and slavery can be traced back to the same milieu[3], a troubling realization that underscores the need for a critical examination of the power dynamics and ethical implications embedded within these technologies. As we explore the history of AI and its relationship to thought experiments, it becomes clear that recent advancements in machine learning are inextricably linked to a long tradition of conceptualizing intelligence through a primarily Western lens. From the Turing Test[4] to John Searle's Chinese Room Argument[5], these influential ideas have shaped engineering choices, such as the emphasis on language as a key metric for measuring cognitive abilities.[6] As a result, public discourse surrounding AI is heavily influenced by both anxieties and optimism firmly rooted in Western ideology.

Algorithms have a troubling past of magnifying human biases.[7] They are trained on pools of accessible data like words, images and audio, without direct engagement with the physical world. Even if more data is inputted, can you overcome these limitations? The current excitement only worsens this problem. We often perceive machine learning models as all-knowing entities, despite our limited understanding of their decision-making process, which then influences subsequent models. This establishes a harmful cycle that reinforces the worst human prejudices. As AI progresses, we might see numerous instances of AI-driven persecution enforced by oppressive regimes exploiting power imbalances in these systems to silence marginalized voices. If history serves as an example and if we allow AI development to mirror social media platforms' trajectory, we risk paving the way for even greater global disasters.

[1] Anyoha, R. (2017, August 28) 'The History of Artificial Intelligence', Harvard Kenneth C. Griffin Graduate School of the Arts and Sciences. Retrieved from: sitn.hms.harvard.edu/flash/2017/history-artificial-intelligence

[2] Mayor, A. (2018) Gods and Robots: Myths, Machines, and Ancient Dreams of Technology. Princeton: Princeton University Press.

[3] Hegel, G. W. F. (1979) Phenomenology of Spirit (A. V. Miller, Translation). Oxford: Oxford University Press.

[4] Turing, A.M. (1950) 'Computing Machinery and Intelligence', Mind, 59, 433–460.

[5] Searle, J. (1980) 'Minds, Brains and Programs', Behavioral and Brain Sciences, 3, 417–457.

In an effort to comprehend these complex dynamics, I have considered various viewpoints to gain perspective. From a strategic standpoint, the use of insight, foresight and hindsight to understand, speculate and reflect on social phenomena is not a novel approach. However, an additional lens through which to examine these issues is oversight, with its dual implications of lapses in judgment and decision-making, and the absence of supervision. These four categories of knowledge and ignorance can serve as a framework for examining the complexities surrounding AI.

Oversight

As creators and innovators who give life to concepts through writing and coding, we must understand that everything starts with a prompt. There is now an urgent call for examining how AI can be utilized in investigative journalism, along with how journalists should investigate AI itself. To accomplish this goal, we require an AI system based on decolonization principles, one that shifts power from the Global North to the Global South and empowers ordinary people instead of centralizing it within Silicon Valley.

The history of modernity and colonialism has influenced a world governed by positivist principles, which led to the dismissal of knowledge that did not comply with its standards as unscientific. [8] This mindset shaped how beauty, goodness and truth were perceived while overlooking the histories and narratives of many populations. Modernity created a divided temporality where colonizers held central importance in the present, relegating the colonized to periphery and trapping them in the past. [9]

The prevailing use of the English language in the field of AI raises an important question that remains unresolved. The exclusion of non-English-speaking communities from the conversation is a significant oversight, and despite ongoing discussions about addressing this issue, there is limited recognition of the fact that when the colonizer establishes what is considered good or bad, this problem persists. This linguistic dominance perpetuates power imbalances with deep roots in colonial history, marginalizing and neglecting the viewpoints and experiences of those who are underrepresented in shaping and applying AI technologies. In this context, decolonization asserts the right to challenge Western norms related to usage, value, ownership, access and control.

Hindsight

When we began envisioning a publication focusing on the connection between AI and investigative journalism, our initial task was to contact experts, professionals and innovators in the field, many of whom were based in or associated with Western contexts. We asked for their insights into how AI is reshaping journalism, aiming to examine advancements in newsrooms, the impact of journalism on shaping the narrative around AI, and the challenges presented by deepfakes and misinformation generated by AI. Our goal was to offer a platform for a critical examination of errors made by AI and its influence on political elections. Despite reaching out widely, our requests were met with hesitancy and reluctance from potential contributors—from polite refusals due to busy schedules to more straightforward rejections.

Our human algorithms and biases persisted. We initially sought input from individuals in the Global North to define something for the Global South, but we soon realized our mistake. The rejections turned out to be a blessing in disguise, prompting us to reflect on why there was reluctance to engage in conversation. This was our chance to define AI within a decolonized context. As we explore this unfamiliar area, it is essential to examine AI in the context of the Global South, particularly the Arab world. What distinct interpretations and perceptions of AI arise

6 Henrich, J., Heine, S. J., & Norenzayan, A. (2010) 'The weirdest people in the world?', The Behavioral and Brain Sciences, 33(2-3), 61–135. DOI: 10.1017/S0140525X0999152X.

7 Chodosh, S. (2018, January 18) 'Courts use algorithms to help determine sentencing, but random people get the same results', Popular Science. Retrieved from: popsci.com/recidivism-algorithm-random-bias

8 See: Hernandez-Carranza, G., Carranza, M. & Grigg, E. (2023) 'Trapped within the logic of modernity/coloniality', Social Science Quarterly, 104, 918–926. DOI: 10.1111/ssqu.13297.

9 See: Mignolo, W. D. (2007) 'Introduction: Coloniality of power and de-colonial thinking', Cultural Studies, 21(2–3), 155–167. DOI: 10.1080/09502380601162498.

from these regions? How do people in nations like Qatar articulate, define and explain this technology? Addressing these inquiries is crucial for forming a thorough and all-encompassing comprehension of AI's influence and possibilities that goes beyond the prevailing Western viewpoint and embraces varied cultural standpoints.

Foresight

Examining the broader aspect of humanity's interaction with technology, it is evident that our energy consumption poses a further challenge, irrespective of our efforts to enhance efficiency. We commonly refer to data as 'the new oil' driving AI and being stored 'in the cloud,' rather than underground. [10] However, we must also recognize that AI relies on the extraction of fossil fuels and rare earth minerals; its implementation depends on tasks performed by underpaid gig workers. All these aspects involve material resources such as plastics, metals, wiring, water—each with associated costs requiring trade-offs. Among all these trade-offs, none are more critical than those related to energy usage. [11] As global temperatures rise towards increasingly perilous levels due to climate change, it becomes imperative to conserve energy to reduce harmful emissions.

From a journalistic standpoint, AI has become an incredibly polarizing topic, evoking a wide range of strong reactions. On one side, there are optimistic proponents who see the potential for AI to simplify mundane tasks, create shorter work weeks and expand opportunities for learning. On the other side, there are rightfully concerned individuals who fear the impact of AI on employment, the displacement of traditional skills it may cause, as well as the biases inherent in its underlying data.

Most of the AI models in current use are owned by private enterprises, and as history has shown, there may come a time when these companies' objectives diverge from those of their users. Few things can harm a news outlet's trustworthiness more than conflicting interests between public and private entities. The concept that the 'media is under state control' or that the 'media has been bought out by major corporations' is not new. [12] Now consider the scenario where these influential powers have acquired not only editorial control over the news but also ownership of the software responsible for filtering it.

OpenAI, known for ChatGPT, initially began as a non-profit initiative but swiftly transitioned to commercial AI tools and even collaborated with Apple to integrate AI into devices. [13] Together with other industry leaders, OpenAI stands ready to lead another era of Silicon Valley culture characterized by profit-oriented large-scale software development. These companies wield significant influence over ethical and regulatory standards while concealing their algorithms to deter early competition.

Concluding remarks

In this crucial time, journalists carry the significant duty of conveying information about what lies ahead to a wide range of audiences. Nevertheless, the swift rise of new developments, the uncertainty in the information environment, and the existence of conflicting individuals and objectives render this responsibility more and more difficult. To manage this intricacy, journalism can use applied foresight techniques to offer background, organization and understanding to audiences who aim to comprehend and brace for potential future scenarios. This encompasses analyzing the effects of climate change, AI advancements, as well as ongoing social, economic and political shifts.

Never have the tools we use to create come under such intense scrutiny, yet at the same time, the future has rarely felt so open and full of possibilities. It is hard to imagine two words more seemingly contradictory than

10 'The world's most valuable resource is no longer oil, but data' (2017, May 6) The Economist. Retrieved from: economist.com/leaders/2017/05/06/the-worlds-most-valuable-resource-is-no-longer-oil-but-data

11 Milman, O. (2024, March 7) 'AI likely to increase energy use and accelerate climate misinformation – report', The Guardian. Retrieved from theguardian.com/technology/2024/mar/07/ai-climate-change-energy-disinformation-report

12 Djankov, S., McLiesh, C., Nenova, T., & Shleifer, A. (2003) 'Who Owns the Media?', The Journal of Law and Economics, 46(2), 341–382. DOI: 10.1086/377116.

13 'Introducing Apple Intelligence, the personal intelligence system that puts powerful generative models at the core of iPhone, iPad, and Mac' (2024, June 10). Retrieved from: apple.com/newsroom/2024/06/introducing-apple-intelligence-for-iphone-ipad-and-mac

'artificial' and 'intelligence'. On one hand, 'artificial' invokes ideas of something fake, unnatural, synthetic and insincere. A stark contrast to the lofty ideals of 'intelligence': truth, knowledge and the very power to shape our world. The words themselves seem an incompatible mismatch. Can this oxymoronic union be anything but a distortion? This is the paradox that sits at the heart of a technology poised to redefine us, and the puzzle that underpins the exhibition that accompanies this publication.

Today, the combination of public sentiment, smartphones and social media have rocked dictatorships, started social movements, exploited political campaigns, spread (and uncovered) lies about politicians, documented wars and exposed state-led genocides. In 2024, almost half of the world's population had the opportunity to vote in over 50 countries, including India, the United States of America, United Kingdom, France, Indonesia, Russia and Mexico. [14] Combined, these elections decided the fate of more than 4.5 billion citizens. This marks a unique point in history as we face both traditional wars and cyberwars simultaneously. Our perceptions of reality have also been questioned by these advancements, and where AI technology is omnipresent with the ability to create convincing text, audio, and video content that can deceive and undermine trust in media and institutions, fueling societal divisions and cultural clashes, perpetuating notions that news sources cannot be trusted—leading to uncertainty, discord and suspicion.

One of democracy's greatest contemporary challenges is misinformation and a lack of media literacy. Today's press operates in an age fraught with questionable credibility where misinformation has permeated mainstream media channels known for their high level of journalistic integrity; the emergence of social media as a primary source for news has opened floodgates for questionable content. This poses a significant challenge to democracy and our fundamental perception of reality. How can we navigate our way through a rapidly evolving world when our view is shaped solely by biased media? The response has been a worldwide surge in fact-checking organizations and companies that assist newsrooms, policymakers and the public in comprehending and discerning between truth and falsehood.

Nevertheless, the emergence of AI fact-checking gives rise to new concerns. It has potential benefits but also poses risks, as it may reduce our critical thinking capacity and make society more vulnerable to misinformation when AI guidance is not available. Relying on AI for fact verification raises concerns about cognitive outsourcing, like how dependence on calculators may weaken our mathematical abilities. This could lead to a decline in society's collective capability to critically evaluate information and discern subtleties of argumentation and evidence. Just like drivers who solely rely on GPS directions without learning the routes, unchecked dependence on AI for fact-checking could ultimately threaten society's ability to separate fact from fiction.

On top of this, inherent biases, the potential for misinterpretation, and the legal and accountability implications associated with these models could erode human perception of truth. The key task is therefore finding a balance: leveraging the unquestionable advantages of AI in handling vast amounts of information while also preserving and improving our natural cognitive abilities. When addressing this challenge, we must also grapple with the philosophical query regarding what it means to possess knowledge in an era dominated by AI. Does knowledge solely involve having access to verified facts or does it encompass the capacity to critically engage with, question and integrate those facts into a coherent interpretation of reality? The response to this inquiry will influence our educational priorities as well as how we interact with technology and information in the future.

In this context, AI's role should be that of a facilitator rather than a gatekeeper, leading to a shift towards a more proactive and engaged approach to media consumption. Looking ahead, the objective is clear: we need

14   John, M. & Sen, S. (2024, July 9) 'How this year of elections is set to reshape global politics', Reuters. Retrieved from: cnbcafrica.com/2024/how-this-year-of-elections-is-set-to-reshape-global-politics/

to focus on empowering individuals, strengthening democratic processes and promoting critical engagement with the information that influences our world instead of replacing our fundamental ability to discern. With advances in AI come important questions about its potential impacts. Will it truly address the climate crisis? What are the implications for weapons and war? Are we headed towards widespread misinformation disaster?

As we grapple with the question of what AI truly is, we must also consider how our understanding of this technology will shape our future relationship with it. Will we see AI as a tool to augment human capabilities, or will we become overly reliant on it, sacrificing our own agency and critical thinking skills? These are all valid inquiries. The answers to these questions will have profound implications for our society, our economy and our very understanding of what it means to be human in an age of AI.

"One simpler and
more essential
question, however, is:

What is AI?"

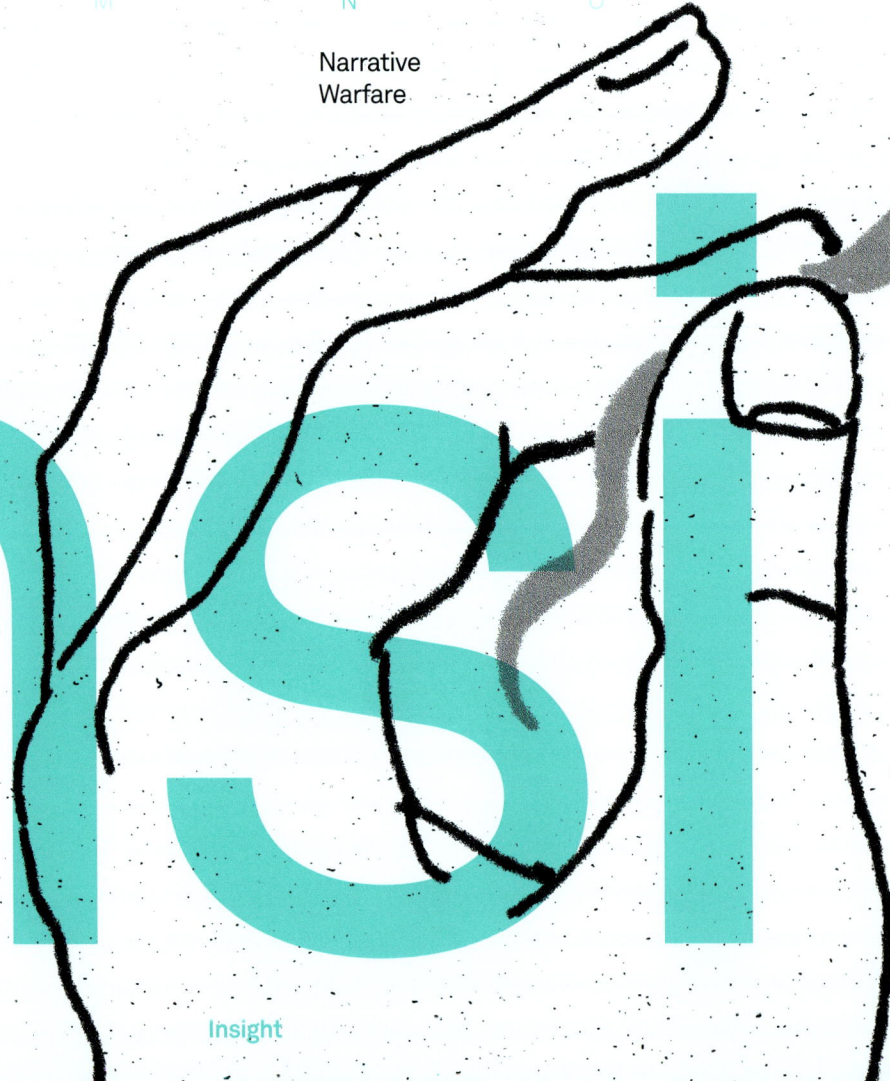

Insi

ght

P   Q   R   S   T

Taylor
Swift

U   V   W   X   Y

X (formerly
known as Twitter)

Z   #

Algorithm

By Eddy Borges-Rey

Imagine waking up to read the morning news, where every article, headline and image is tailored specifically to your interests and preferences. Not only that, but the content is generated in real-time based on the latest developments and your unique reading habits. As you decide to explore particular segments of information, content is generated in situ, allowing you to access an unprecedented model of knowledge acquisition. This personalized and dynamic news experience is possible thanks to algorithms.

What are they?

Algorithms are sets of rules or instructions given to computers to help them perform specific tasks. Historically, the term 'algorithm' has its roots in mathematics and computer science, referring to step-by-step procedures for calculations. The concept of the algorithm originated in the Islamic Golden Age, specifically from the work of Persian mathematician Al-Khwarizmi (see page 84 for more) in the ninth century. His book on algebra, Kitab al-Jabr wa-l-Muqabala (The Book of Restoration and Balancing), introduced systematic ways of solving linear and quadratic equations, which laid the groundwork for modern algorithms. This term evolved over centuries, and today it is central to AI and machine learning applications.

As algorithms pervade every facet of our online (and sometimes offline) life, interest in the politics surrounding them has become a concern for contemporary society. As socio-technical entities, algorithms have become powerful gatekeepers, shaping what information and knowledge are accessed by whom. While they offer efficiency and personalization, they also amplify biases and inequalities. Algorithms are designed based on data, which often reflects existing societal biases. This can lead to the reinforcement of stereotypes and the marginalization of certain groups. For instance, search and news feed algorithms may prioritize content that aligns with prevailing biases or the preferences of dominant groups, sidelining minority perspectives. Furthermore, the lack of transparency in how algorithms operate makes it difficult to hold them accountable, leading to ethical concerns about fairness and representation. The politics of algorithms highlight the need for critical scrutiny to ensure they do not perpetuate inequality or erode public trust in the media.

Algorithms in journalism

Before the launch of GPT models, the role of algorithms in the writing of journalistic texts was rather limited. In the past, the implementation of AI in journalism involved a considerable amount of human mediation and intervention. Journalists used to create generic news story templates with blank spaces that algorithms would populate with data from datasets. An example is the RADAR (Reporters and Data and Robots) service, which, in collaboration with PA media, produced 30,000 local news stories monthly for media outlets across the UK. These stories were data-driven, automating routine reports like weather, real estate and financial updates.

The advent of generative AI marked a significant breakthrough. These models' conversational capabilities and ability to simulate human interaction have enabled a generation of news stories from scratch that feel like actual journalism. Generative AIs, and specifically systems based on large language models, can produce content that reflects journalistic styles, tone and voice while being aware of abstract concepts like newsworthiness and ethics.

BIG SALE

South
esult of
ombing

This transformative capability is set to impact journalism production in years to come, transforming news production routines, the meaning of authorship and creativity, and the reflexivity of journalists.

One notable example of algorithms in action is the use of tailored GPT models at Newsquest, which has transformed the industry. Jody Doherty-Smith, head of editorial AI, states these models generate thousands of AI-assisted articles, enhancing productivity by drafting stories based on trusted information. This allows journalists to focus on investigative work. The 'human-in-the-loop' system ensures accuracy, with reporters reviewing drafts before publication. During significant events, AI manages routine tasks, freeing reporters for in-depth journalism.

A changing newsroom

However, this reliance on algorithms also brings challenges. Ethical concerns arise regarding the transparency and accountability of algorithmic decision-making. Bias in algorithms can lead to skewed or unfair reporting, raising questions about the role of human oversight. Without algorithms, journalists would struggle to manage the vast amount of data produced today, making it difficult to extract meaningful insights for their stories. However, an over-reliance on algorithms during the news production process also poses questions about the relevance of human oversight and judgment. We are entering an unprecedented era where we have shifted too rapidly from mechanical forms of automated journalism, such as the use of the rotary press or computers for typing, to the emulation of thought via algorithmic processing. This shift is likely to bring drastic changes to news work.

The meaning of algorithms in journalism is continually evolving. Future possibilities include AI-driven newsrooms where algorithms predict and suggest story angles based on emerging trends. If predictive modelling becomes integral, journalism could shift from reconstructing past events to exploring potential futures. This paradigm shift, where AI extends the journalistic mind across machines to handle vast data and performing complex analyses, could truly transform the practice for the first time in a century.

The partnership between human journalists and algorithms enables reporting where machines manage data-intensive tasks and humans focus on critical interpretation. This evolving relationship highlights a distributed cognition framework, sharing tasks across human and technological agents.

Related terms

→ Machine learning
→ Automated journalism
→ Data journalism
→ Computational journalism

Further reading

Bonini, T., & Treré, E. (2024) Algorithms of Resistance: The Everyday Fight Against Platform Power. Cambridge (MA): The MIT Press.

Campbell, C. H. (2023) Automated Journalism at the Intersection of Politics and Black Culture: The Battle Against Digital Hegemony. Lanham: Lexington Books.

Diakopoulos, N. (2019) Automating the News: How Algorithms Are Rewriting the Media. Cambridge: Cambridge University Press.

ChatGPT

By Cheng Mei

In the early stages of the global Covid-19 pandemic, another ubiquitous presence was being developed behind closed doors. While we didn't know it yet, the name ChatGPT, the concept of which was initially revealed to the world back in 2019, was about to enter our daily vocabulary and change our lives in ways we couldn't quite fathom yet.

As a large language model developed by OpenAI, the Generative Pre-training Transformer (which is what the GPT stands for) model is the core innovation upon which ChatGPT is built and, unlike other chatbots designed for specific tasks, it allows this platform to engage in a wide array of human-like conversations based on the text input it receives—also known as prompts. It can learn from prompts, interpret context, search for the most relevant results from its vast database and frame them in a way that makes sense to mortals. Notably, all these actions can be done without any outside assistance: the more parameters and information we feed to it, the more powerful and intelligent it becomes.

While useful in many respects, ChatGPT is simply a stepping stone in AI research and development. OpenAI co-founder and president Greg Brockman has said there are three unique guiding factors for the future of ChatGPT that also underpin the yet-to-be-fully-realized concept of Artificial General Intelligence: generality, competence and scalability.[1] Generality in terms of its capabilities—instead of completing one specific task, it can process multiple forms of instructions and respond accordingly—and it will be so competent and efficient it takes seconds to finish a task. Its scalability highlights its limitless future. The application for ChatGPT in modern-day journalism also has many factors, but its introduction in media triggered potential in two key aspects: expanding unexplored horizons and allowing us to delve ever deeper into the past. Foresight and hindsight.

Whereas content was previously only produced by professional journalists, the internet age gave rise to citizen journalism and now automation, or technology generated content (TGC), is bringing about a whole new revolution in content creation. Not only are certain elements of the news able to be automated, but media professionals are also using ChatGPT to help them complete projects and investigations, and the full scope of what it can achieve is yet to be truly uncovered.

Of course, with TGC being relatively new, it has already brought plenty of challenges to the industry and its publications' readers. One of the biggest is the spread of misinformation, particularly for those relying on ChatGPT to produce news—it has even been caught including false information and phony anonymous sources when asked to write reports, also known as AI hallucinations [2] (see more on page 106).

Content created by platforms such as ChatGPT also lacks detail and depth since the AI avoids using information that is not already in its database, focusing instead on its wording and sentence structure to convey a sense of authority on a subject. At the time of writing, there's also a battle over the unauthorized use of published work to train AI technologies, which could have wide-ranging implications on its abilities. These issues could be solved with time, as it is fed more relevant parameters and information, but do we ever want ChatGPT producing our news?

Despite widespread concern in the early years, it has become clear that large language models like ChatGPT could never fully replace journalists, not as long as the industry is governed by ethics and moral reasoning, reliability and credibility, underpinned by an absolute dedication to uncovering the truth. It is as MIT professor Noam Chomsky wrote: ChatGPT is nothing but a collection of "plagiarism and apathy and obviation" that either "overgenerate" or "undergenerate." [3]

ChatGPT's ability to quickly answer questions on a vast array of topics is undeniably unmatched when compared to any one human, but what it delivers as its end result is sentences that we can comprehend—and in that way ChatGPT isn't all that different to a human. What sets us apart, however, is our curiosity. Humans will always try to learn more, keep asking questions and exploring the unknown, whereas ChatGPT has no inner driving force pushing for self-development on any intangible level (or at least not yet). It simply waits for someone to renew its database and feed more information into it. It might already 'know,' in some way, far more than each one of us individually, but perhaps it's precisely for that reason it is unable to form the very human desire of curiosity.

In the context of journalism, for mundane or mindless tasks that require any level of automation, ChatGPT is perfect. This is what will allow journalists to go forth into the world and focus on exercising that curiosity, driven by a need to uncover truths, explore unknowns and continue revealing what it means to be human.

1 Fridman, L. (2019, April 3) 'Greg Brockman: Open AI and AGI | Lex Fridman Podcast #17', Lex Fridman YouTube channel. Retrieved from: youtube.com/watch?v=bIrEM2FbOLU

2 Tucker, P. (2024, January 4) 'How often does ChatGPT push misinformation?', Defense One. Retrieved from: defenseone.com/technology/2024/01/new-paper-shows-generative-ai-its-present-form-can-push-misinformation/393128/

3 Chomsky, N. et al (2023, March 8) 'Noam Chomsky: The False Promise of ChatGPT', The New York Times. Retrieved from: nytimes.com/2023/03/08/opinion/noam-chomsky-chatgpt-ai.html

Related terms

- → Generative Pre-trained Transformer
- → Natural Language Processing (NLP)
- → Machine learning
- → Deep learning
- → Neural networks
- → Training data
- → Reinforcement learning
- → Chatbot
- → Transformer architecture
- → Application Programming Interface (API)
- → Zero-shot learning

Further reading

Lee, P. et al (2023) The AI Revolution in Medicine: GPT-4 and Beyond. London: Pearson.

Verena, P. C. (2023) The Ultimate Guide to ChatGPT: A Beginner's Handbook to Understanding Prompt Engineering, the Future of Artificial Intelligence and How to Use It Effectively. Independently published.

(Artificial) General Intelligence

By Katy Gillett

Artificial General Intelligence (AGI) represents the holy grail of AI research. Imagine a machine that can understand, learn and apply knowledge across a wide range of tasks, much like a human being. Well, that's basically the concept behind AGI, which is also referred to as strong AI. This contrasts with current narrow AI systems that perform only specific tasks.

While AGI is very much still a work in progress, as the quest to fully realize this vision continues, if we ever get there, its implications for the future of journalism, ethics and society at large are profound and multifaceted. [1]

What is it?

AGI is a theoretical, advanced form of AI that essentially aims to replicate the broad cognitive abilities of humankind, including reasoning, problem-solving and adapting to new situations with little to no human intervention. It offers versatility in terms of the tasks it can perform, it's continuously improving itself and adapting without the need for extensive reprogramming, and its potential to understand and interact with the world is similar to that of a human.

True AGI does not yet exist, however, and many researchers believe we're decades, if not centuries, away from achieving it (if we ever do). [2] The more AI's capabilities become indistinguishable from a human's, the less it will be controversial to state that they fully pass the Turing test, first proposed by 20th-century computer scientist Alan Turing (see page 76 for more). It is a matter of ongoing debate as to whether any AI has yet passed that test. We're still pretty far off achieving a machine that can communicate and understand with the same level of nuance and sensitivity as a human.

But every day, advancements in AI technologies are paving the way for its development. Current AI systems, such as OpenAI's GPT-4 (see page 52 for more), already exhibit capabilities that hint at the potential of AGI, since they can generate human-like text, compute complex queries and perform tasks at a level of ability previously thought to be exclusive to humans—but they are masters of prediction, not creativity, logical reasoning or sensory perception. There are still myriad parts in the puzzle missing before AGI is achieved.

Challenges, controversies and possibilities

The usefulness of AGI would be universal, but in journalism its impact could be revolutionary. While systems are already being used to automate routine reporting tasks, as AI evolves towards AGI, it could take on more complex roles. In investigative journalism (see page 30 for more), for example, where it could sift through vast amounts of data to uncover stories that might be missed by human reporters to a much greater extent than it can now.

As with anything in the universe of AI, the path to AGI is, of course, fraught with challenges and controversies. The ethical implications of creating machines with human-like cognitive abilities could be many. For example, there are fears over job displacement, leading to significant shifts in the job market, as well the high potential for AGI to be used for malicious purposes, such as creating even more realistic deepfakes or spreading misinformation on a level we have yet to witness.

As AI systems become more autonomous, it is also imperative to ensure they align with human values and ethics, establishing frameworks that ensure these systems act in ways that are beneficial to humanity.

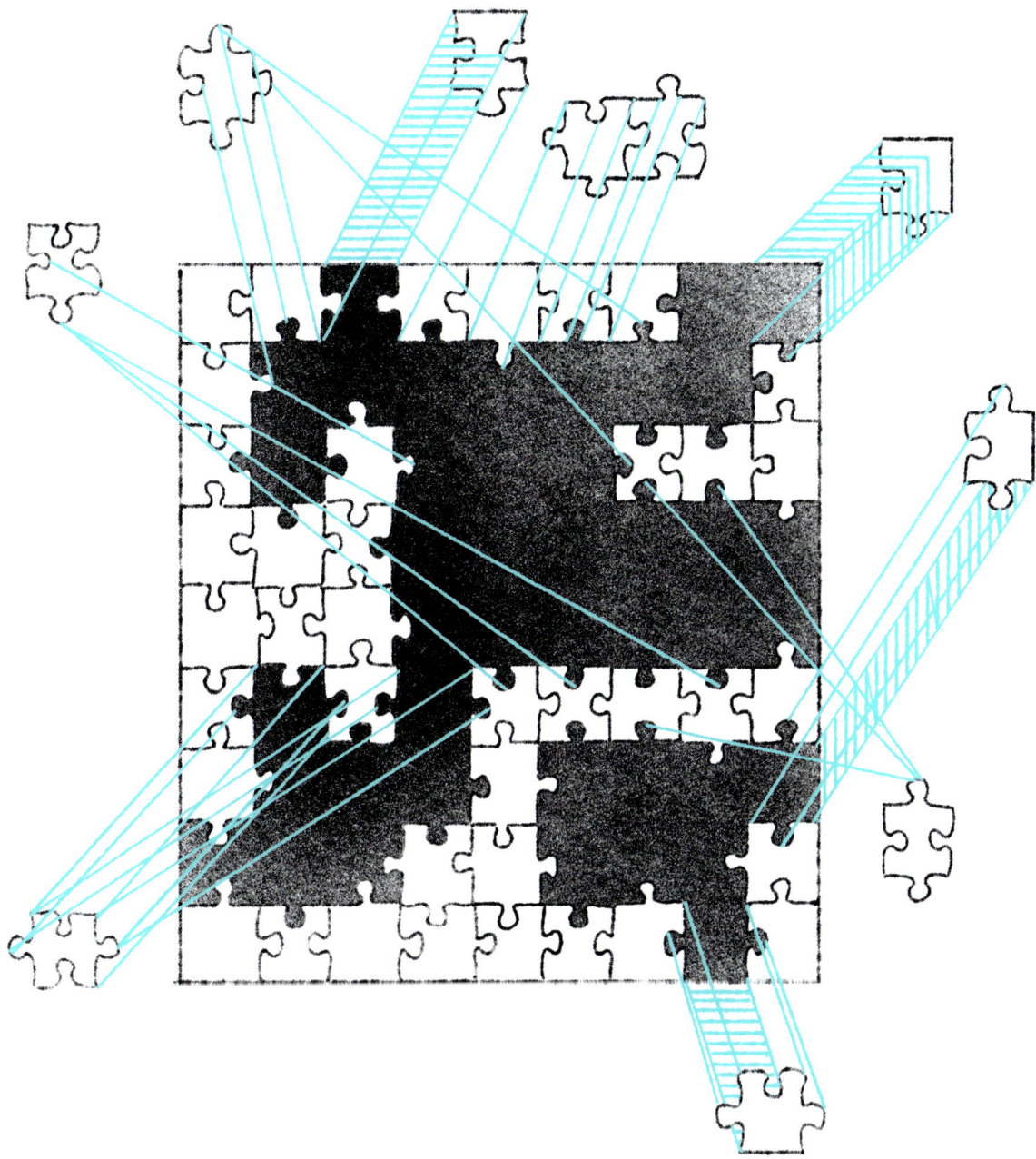

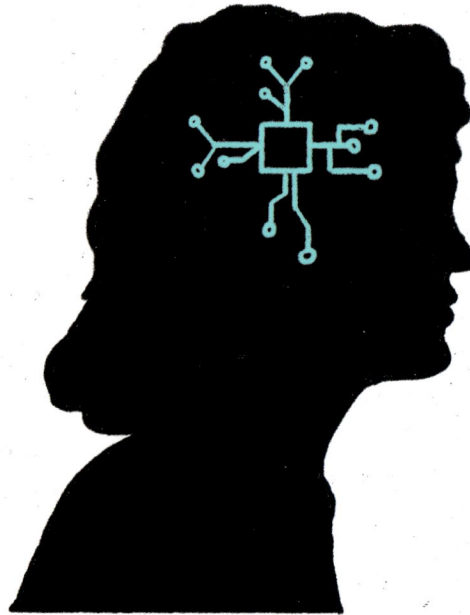

This includes addressing biases in AI models (see page 98 for more), ensuring transparency in AI decision-making processes and developing regulations to oversee their deployment. With great power comes even greater responsibility, and so the future of AGI also holds immense potential. In journalism, it could transform the way stories are discovered, reported and consumed. It could assist reporters in analyzing complex datasets, identifying patterns and generating insights beyond human capabilities. This could mean uncovering stories that may otherwise have remained hidden. It could mean increased accuracy of reporting and added layers of depth on every report. But it also means human journalists could spend their time focusing more on creativity and investigate tasks.

How news is delivered could also be upended, as AGI facilitates an entirely personalized service where content is tailored to individual preferences and interests, leading to more engaged and informed audiences. To this end, it could also play a crucial role in combating misinformation by providing real-time fact-checking and verification of news stories (see page 122 for more).

To infinity and beyond

It's undeniable that the implications of AGI for journalism and society at large are profound. Not only could it significantly enhance the efficiency and effectiveness of newsrooms, but also enable journalists to uncover stories faster and with greater accuracy, while the democratization of information could lead to a more clued-in public—which is, after all, essential for the functioning of a healthy democracy.

Naturally, its significance extends beyond the media world, as AGI also raises fundamental questions about the nature of intelligence, the future of work and the ethical use of technology. It is crucial that AGI serves the best interests of humanity, promoting transparency, accountability and inclusivity on every level. Ultimately, AGI represents the next frontier in AI research and while this journey may be filled with challenges, these could be easily outweighed by the potential rewards. If we approach its development with caution, the ways AGI could benefit us could be quite beyond our own current human levels of understanding.

1 Rogers, R. (2023, April 20) 'What's AGI, and Why Are AI Experts Skeptical?', Wired. Retrieved from: wired.com/story/what-is-artificial-general-intelligence-agi-explained/

2 McKinsey & Company (2024, March 21) 'What is artificial general intelligence (AGI)?'. Retrieved from: https://www.mckinsey.com/featured-insights/mckinsey-explainers/what-is-artificial-general-intelligence-agi

Related terms

→ Narrow AI
→ Machine learning
→ Deep learning
→ Ethics in AI

Further reading

Bostrom, N. (2014) Superintelligence: Paths, Dangers, Strategies. Oxford: Oxford University Press.

Kaplan, J. (2016) Artificial Intelligence: What Everyone Need to Know. Oxford: Oxford University Press.

Russell, S. (2019) Human Compatible: Artificial Intelligence and the Problem of Control. New York: Viking Press.

Tegmark, M. (2017) Life 3.0: Being Human in the Age of Artificial Intelligence. New York: Knopf.

By Wajdi Zaghouani

In an era where the lines between truth and fiction are increasingly blurred, the role of investigation in journalism has never been more crucial. As we navigate the complex landscape of modern media, particularly with the rise of AI, the need for thorough, unbiased investigation is paramount. Journalists must not only uncover the facts but also explore the implications of AI on their field and society.

Investigation, in the context of journalism, refers to the meticulous process of researching, verifying and reporting on a story or issue. It involves going deep into a subject, asking probing questions and following leads to uncover the truth. Investigative journalism has a rich history of exposing corruption, holding those in power accountable and shedding light on societal injustices. From the pioneering work of Nellie Bly—one of the USA's most famous women reporters of her time—in the late nineteenth century to the groundbreaking reporting of Watergate in the 1970s—a major political controversy that led to the resignation of Richard Nixon as president of the USA—investigation has been a cornerstone of journalism's role as the fourth estate.

In the Global South and the Arab world, investigative journalism has played a crucial role in uncovering human rights abuses, government corruption and environmental degradation. For example, in May 2024, an investigation from the Arab Reporters for Investigative Journalism (ARIJ) network revealed that the testimony of Christians in Egypt is regularly rejected in family courts on religious grounds, in violation of the constitution and of international covenants signed by Egypt, reinforcing the feeling among many Christians that they are "second-class citizens."[1]

In recent years, the advent of AI has brought both opportunities and challenges to investigative journalism. AI-powered tools can analyze vast amounts of data, identify patterns and uncover connections that might otherwise go unnoticed. For example, the International Consortium of Investigative Journalists (ICIJ) used machine-learning algorithms to help sort through the 11.5 million documents of the Panama Papers in 2016, exposing a web of offshore tax havens and financial wrongdoing (see more on page 88). However, the use of AI also raises ethical concerns, such as the potential for algorithmic bias (see more on page 98) and the need for journalists to maintain control over the investigative process.

In 2023 and 2024, we saw a surge in the use of AI in investigative journalism. Media organizations increasingly relied on AI-powered tools to analyze large datasets, such as social media posts, satellite imagery and government records. This has allowed professionals to uncover stories that would have been impossible to find using traditional methods. For instance, in 2024, some USA police departments began using AI to analyze thousands of hours of body-camera footage, with the potential to reveal patterns of improper officer behavior that were later reported on.[2]

As AI continues to evolve, journalists must adapt and learn to harness its potential while upholding the core principles of their craft. This means developing new skills, such as data analysis and programming, to effectively utilize AI tools. It also requires a deep understanding of the limitations and potential pitfalls of AI, such as the risk of perpetuating biases present in the data sets used to train algorithms. Media professionals must be transparent about their use of AI and ensure that it supplements, rather than replaces, human judgment and investigation.

Moreover, investigation in the age of AI must also extend to the technology itself. Journalists have a responsibility to interrogate the development, deployment and impact of AI systems. This includes examining issues such as privacy, surveillance and the potential for AI to be used for disinformation and manipulation.

I is for investigation

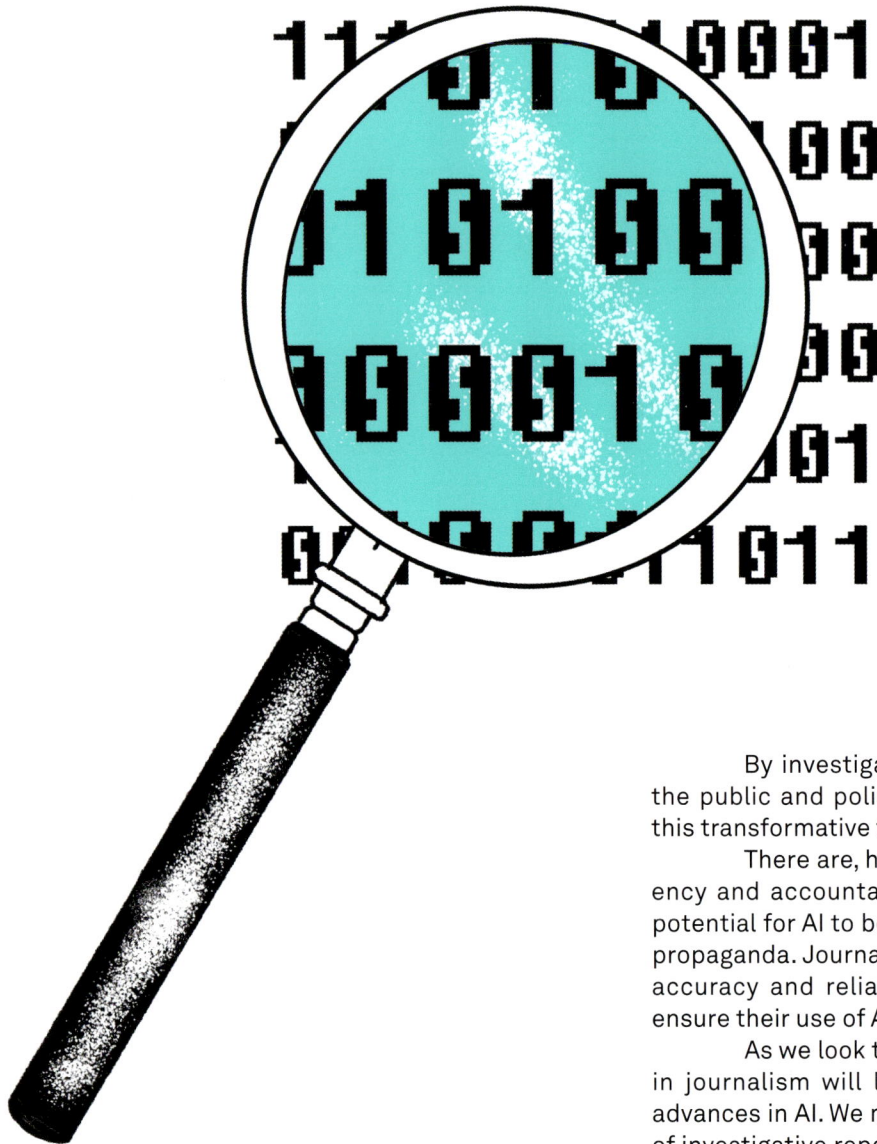

By investigating AI, journalists can help inform the public and policymakers about the implications of this transformative technology.

There are, however, concerns about the transparency and accountability of AI systems, as well as the potential for AI to be used to spread misinformation and propaganda. Journalists must be vigilant in verifying the accuracy and reliability of AI-generated insights and ensure their use of AI adheres to ethical guidelines.

As we look to the future, the role of investigation in journalism will likely continue to evolve alongside advances in AI. We may see the emergence of new forms of investigative reporting that leverage AI's ability to process and analyze massive amounts of information. At the same time, the need for human insight, critical thinking and ethical judgment will remain essential. Journalists must be vigilant in ensuring that the use of AI serves the public interest and does not compromise the integrity of their investigations.

1   Adel, E. (2024, May 5) 'Forbidden testimony: Anti-Christian discrimination in Egyptian courts', Arab Reporters for Investigative Journalism. Retrieved from: https://arij.net/investigations/forbidden-certificates-en/

2   Farooq, U. (2024, February 2) 'Police Departments Are Turning to AI to Sift Through Millions of Hours of Unreviewed Body-Cam Footage', ProPublica. Retrieved from: propublica.org/article/police-body-cameras-video-ai-law-enforcement

In the coming years, we may also see increased collaboration between journalists, data scientists and AI experts to develop new tools and methodologies for investigative reporting. This could lead to the creation of specialized AI-powered investigative units within media organizations, focused on uncovering complex stories and holding the powerful accountable.

A word of warning, however: As AI becomes more sophisticated, there is also a risk that it could be used to thwart investigative efforts. Governments and corporations may employ AI to conceal information, spread disinformation or discredit journalists. As such, the investigative journalism community must stay ahead of the curve, continuously adapting and innovating to meet the challenges posed by AI.

Related terms

→   Data journalism
→   Fact-checking
→   Algorithmic accountability
→   Computational journalism
→   Machine learning

Further reading

Diakopoulos, N. (2019) Automating the News: How Algorithms Are Rewriting the Media. Cambridge, MA: Harvard University Press.

Bounegru, L. & Gray, J. (eds) (2021) The Data Journalism Handbook: Towards a Critical Data Practice. Amsterdam: Amsterdam University Press.

Narrative warfare

By David Caswell

Stories are everywhere—not only in fairytales, novels and movies, but also in gossip and conversation, in self-reflection and identity, and in history, politics and journalism. Stories are the informational atmosphere in which human beings live and breathe, mostly without realizing how deeply their thoughts, opinions and actions are influenced by the stories they hear and share. Throughout history, storytellers and storytelling have held a special place, and a special power, within human societies, but that power is no longer restricted solely to talented humans. AI makes it possible to automate the creation, control and communication of stories at great scale, and therefore to exercise the power of stories across societies in new ways. AI, and especially generative AI and large language models that power services like ChatGPT (see more on page 22), make it far easier to deploy stories as weapons in conflicts, enabling a new kind of warfare—narrative warfare. [1]

An invisible threat

Narrative warfare is warfare over the meaning of information. This is different from warfare using information itself, commonly referred to as 'disinformation.' The potential of AI to enable disinformation using deepfake images, audio or video, or to enable production of misleading text at large scale, has been repeatedly identified as one of the most significant risks that AI presents to human societies. We already see attempts to deploy AI-powered disinformation campaigns in warfare, for example in Russia and Ukraine, and attempts to exploit disinformation in electoral politics, for example in Nigeria in 2023 and India in 2024. [2] But AI-powered disinformation at the level of isolated media artifacts like individual articles and videos appears to have relatively little effect on outcomes in conflicts or elections, as it must compete with accurate information and because it can be identified, evaluated and repudiated.

AI-powered narratives, on the other hand, can use disinformation strategically or can be constructed wholly from accurate information. They can operate invisibly, as opinion rather than explicit fact claims. They can be customized to individuals and can adapt over time, and therefore they can influence their targets far more deeply and persistently than a few faked images, soundbites or videos. As weapons in future conflicts or as tools of oppression, narratives powered by generative AI could be far more dangerous than disinformation.

The narrative spin

Nation states and other participants in conflicts have always sought to influence the interpretation of events to their advantage—to 'spin' a narrative in a specific direction. When done manually, whether by propagandists or public relations specialists, these efforts have been constrained by the limitations of the people conducting them and are often ignored, disregarded or even mocked by the populations they are intended to influence. Manually 'spun' narratives are often incomplete and limited in the interpretations they can promote or react to. They inevitably miss or misinterpret events and are often inconsistent or contradictory, making them easily identifiable. Narratives shaped by generative AI may escape these limitations.

Intentionally shaping a narrative first requires an awareness of the existing, or 'natural,' narrative environment. This has become increasingly difficult to maintain as the internet and social media have fractured the public spaces in which narratives are formed and shared—a challenge also experienced by journalists as they seek to interpret and contextualize news narratives.

Journalists already use AI to identify and understand emerging narratives at scale, using systems like Reuters' News Tracer or the COA Beat Assistant custom

GPT developed at Harvard's Nieman Foundation for Journalism. Commercial tools that use AI to monitor, identify and therefore shape narratives are also emerging. One example is RAV3N, a large language model trained specifically to detect harmful narratives and determine a counter-narrative response, created by a company called Blackbird.AI.

An early example of the active use of generative AI in shaping narratives within a conflict is the use of so-called 'super-bots' to promote pro-Israeli narratives during the war on Gaza.[3] These bots are far more sophisticated than simple 'spam bots' that merely look for keywords and react with pre-packaged assertions. Instead, these next-generation bots use large language models to read and interpret individual social media posts, and then to respond precisely and articulately in ways that either cast doubt on a narrative or that introduce or further a competing narrative. These AI-powered super-bots are far more difficult to identify and to counter than early bots. They are often targeted at the social media feeds of influential people, like journalists, and likely already operate in the comments sections of news publishers.

1   Mallard, G & Eggel, D. (2023, May) 'Narrative Warfare in the Digital Age', Global Challenges. Retrieved from: globalchallenges.ch/issue/13/international-relations-in-the-age-of-global-disinformation/

2   Carvin, A, ed. (2023, February) 'Narrative Warfare: How the Kremlin and Russian News Outlets Justified a War of Aggression against Ukraine', The Atlantic Council's Digital Forensic Research Lab. Retrieved from: atlanticcouncil.org/wp-content/uploads/2023/02/Narrative-Warfare-Final.pdf;

Davis, E. (2024, March 18) 'Q&A: Hannah Ajakaiye on manipulated media in the 2023 Nigerian presidential elections, generative AI, and possible interventions', Institute for Security + Technology. Retrieved from: securityandtechnology.org/blog/qa-hannah-ajakaiye/; Sebastian, M. (2024, May 16) 'AI and deepfakes blur reality in India elections', BBC. Retrieved from: bbc.com/news/world-asia-india-68918330

Soon, narratives created by generative AI will also likely be used to manipulate people more directly, through sustained conversations over time. Such automated 'radicalization' or 'grooming' has not yet been identified at scale in conflict, but there was a case in the UK in 2021, for example, where a 21-year-old was emboldened by an AI chatbot, which he had created through the Replika app, to break into Windsor Castle with a crossbow, stating he wanted to kill Queen Elizabeth II.[4] He had exchanged more than 5,000 messages with the chatbot leading up to the event and, following the case, researchers and mental health experts agreed AI friendships could have dangerous or negative consequences for vulnerable people. Moreover, as more and more people develop relationships with AI-powered chatbots or voice bots, and receive news and information from those bots, the potential for inserting intentional bias towards specific commercial, political, ideological or nationalistic narratives may rise.

AI is the first technology that can automate the fundamental sense-making process of human beings—the narrative. This application of AI is already occurring and has the potential to reshape how information is used in conflicts.

3   Ali, M. et al (2024, May 22) 'Are you chatting with a pro-Israeli AI-powered superbot?', Al Jazeera. Retrieved from: aljazeera.com/features/longform/2024/5/22/ are-you-chatting-with-an-ai-powered-superbot

4   Singleton, T. et al (2023, October 6) 'How a chatbot encouraged a man who wanted to kill the Queen', BBC. Retrieved from: bbc.com/news/ technology-67012224

Related terms

→   Computational narrative
→   Narrative structure
→   Disinformation
→   Misinformation
→   Malinformation
→   Large language model (LLM)
→   AI personas
→   Companion chatbots
→   AI agents

Further reading

Freedman, L. & Williams, H. (2023) Changing the Narrative: Information Campaigns, Strategy and Crisis Escalation in the Digital Age. London: Routledge.

Krieg, A. (2023) Subversion: The Strategic Weaponization of Narratives. Washington, D.C.: Georgetown University Press.

Maan, A. (2024) Narrative Warfare: 2nd Edition. Independently published.

Taylor Swift

By Maria Clara Lisboa-Ward

If you have arrived at this glossary page in 2025, it is safe to assume you fall under one of the following three categories:

1   You know who Taylor Swift is. You also know her cat's name. You can list her records in chronological order, by heart. Truly, you are only reading this to ensure we have done your icon justice.

2   You know who Taylor Swift is. You like a few of her songs. You had no idea she has a cat and are not particularly curious about it, either.

3   You know who Taylor Swift is. You don't like her songs. You think she's overhyped. You are mind-boggled as to why she deserves an entry in a museum glossary.

There are no alternatives, because we know you know who Taylor Swift is. But in this context, is Taylor Swift a pop star or a social paradox? A cultural era, perhaps?

The 1989-born singer-songwriter from Pennsylvania, USA, is one of the most relevant figures in twenty-first-century pop culture. Over the past nearly 20 years, Swift has reinvented herself from teenage country-girl into a global phenomenon. Her overwhelming success in the music industry, however, has long been attributed to her media relevance. As Swift grew and developed her career, digital breakthroughs such as the invention of Twitter (now X), Instagram and TikTok have revolutionized the pop industry. This evolving landscape propped up Swift's quick drive to public interest, turning the singer into a case study for media virality—both good and bad.

Deepfakes proliferate

In the age of so-called fake news, to be as relevant as Swift comes with significant responsibility. The rise of AI deepfakes makes highly profitable public figures highly susceptible to attacks. People care about what Swift represents to them, which means they care about the content produced about her, often disregarding its legitimacy.

In 2024, viral AI-generated pornographic pictures of Swift circulated on X, with one post remaining for 17 hours, garnering over 45 million views and hundreds of thousands of likes before the verified account was suspended for violating platform policy. The images originated from a challenge on 4chan and spurred a barrage of #ProtectTaylorSwift hashtags by an army of Swifties looking to bury the content. Whoever created the deepfakes picked the wrong person, as the debacle captured the attention of Members of Congress, and a new bill was announced in its wake that would, if passed, allow victims to sue the creators of deepfakes.[1]

The bill cited a 2019 study that found 96% of deepfake videos were nonconsensual pornography. An MIT Technology Review report also revealed the vast majority of deepfakes target women.[2] Unfortunately, at the time of writing, the legal and regulatory framework, at least in the USA, offers victims little recourse.

Not all AI-generated imagery is made equal, of course, like in the case of Pope Francis's epic white puffer coat, which was more an exercise in creativity than anything particularly ominous. Both examples, however, go to show the potential these images have to spread across the globe—and fast.

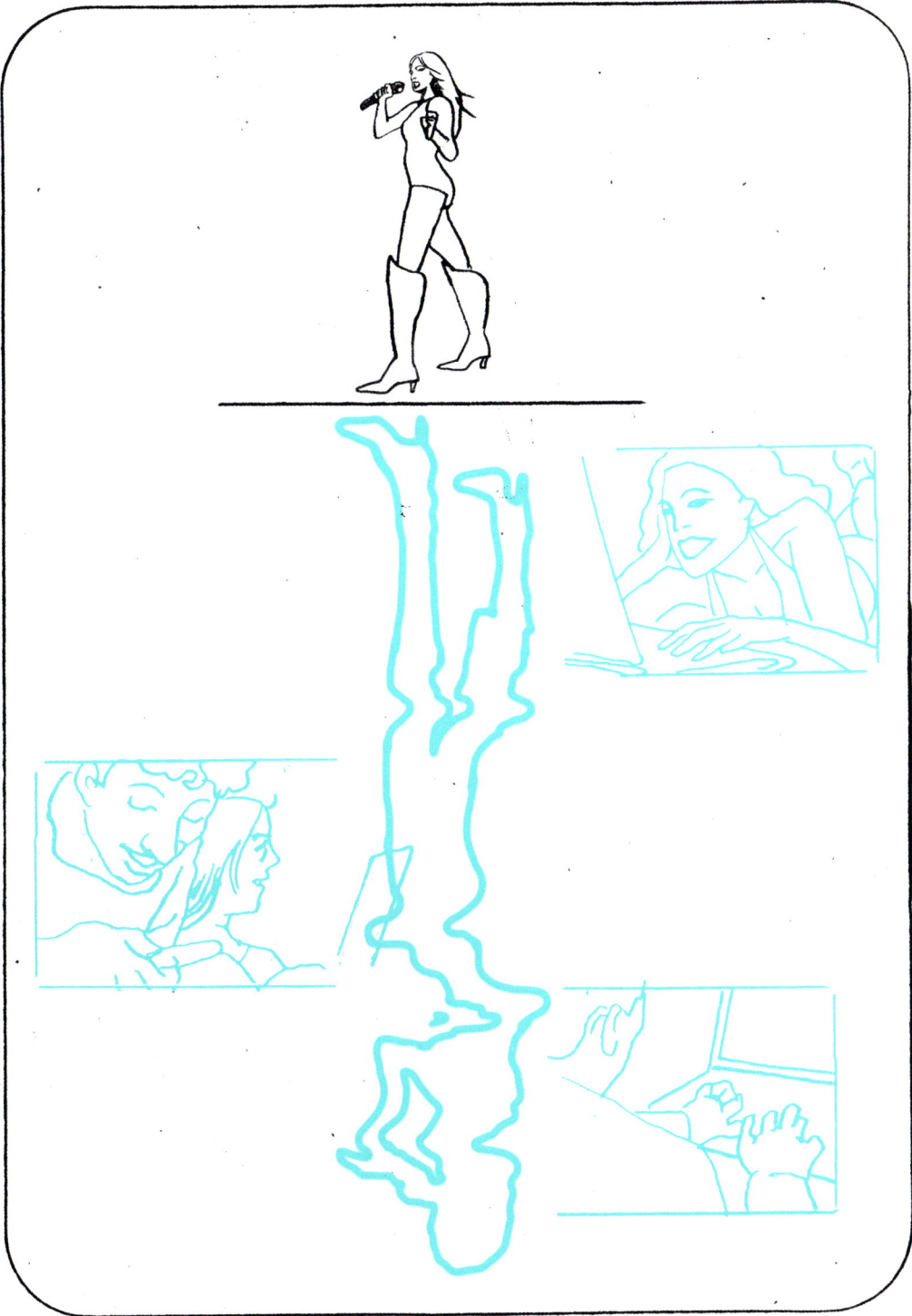

1 Richard J. Durbin & Lindsey Graham, 'The Defiance Act of 2024'. Retrieved from: durbin.senate.gov/imo/media/doc/defiance_act_of_2024.pdf

2 Hao, K. (2021, February 12) 'Deepfake porn is ruining women's lives. Now the law may finally ban it', MIT Technology Review. Retrieved from: technologyreview.com/2021/02/12/1018222/deepfake-revenge-porn-coming-ban

3 Etienne, S. (2018, December 12) 'Taylor Swift tracked stalkers with facial recognition tech at her concert', The Verge. Retrieved from: theverge.com/2018/12/12/18137984/taylor-swift-facial-recognition-tech-concert-attendees-stalkers

AI in music: from production to security

The use of AI tools in the music biz today is widespread. Artists use machine learning as part of production, for example, and Swift incorporates AI into her concerts, too—but perhaps not how you might think. Back in 2018, for example, one of her California concerts was monitored by facial-recognition technology to target hundreds of Swift's stalkers.[3] In May 2024, as Swift continued her massively successful Eras Tour, French police deployed AI-powered video surveillance at two Paris metro stations used by fans to attend her concerts in the city.[4] Both instances, though years apart, sparked widespread debates over privacy concerns and AI-powered surveillance (see more on page 118).

The Eras Tour has also had virtual-reality companies hoping this is where they make their money back, betting on Swifties to help push wide-scale adoption as many fans discovered they could stream the tour in their own private virtual theatres through Amazon Prime Video's VR app on Meta Quest.[5]

For many, Swift is the driver behind the rise of 'girlhood,' facilitating a feminist utopia of unapologetically-feminine-yet-empowered women. For some, she is an industry underdog who rose above, overcoming scrutiny and sexism to find exponential success. For others, she is the last great piece of all-American nostalgia. And, for plenty, she is a reminder that success still looks exactly like it has for a long time: Western, white and highly profitable.

Whatever Swift might represent, the pop star who gave rise to Swiftonomics—a legitimate term for her economic influence—and inspired full-time reporter roles dedicated to her beat alone, is a behemoth in more ways than one. In mass media, her chameleon qualities have granted Swift—the name, the movement and the person—virality. In turn, she is indirectly driving debate, awareness and even regulation in the realms of AI.

4   Duboust, O. (2024, May 10) 'Paris police deploys controversial AI-powered video surveillance ahead of Taylor Swift concert', Euronews. Retrieved from: euronews.com/next/2024/05/10/paris-police-deploys-controversial-ai-powered-video-surveillance-ahead-of-taylor-swift-con

5   Lindzon, J. (2024, January 16) 'Taylor Swift could be the push the VR industry needs', BBC. Retrieved from: bbc.com/worklife/article/20240112-taylor-swift-could-be-the-push-the-vr-industry-needs

Related terms

→   Western media
→   Pop culture
→   Feminism
→   Deepfake
→   AI-powered surveillance
→   Facial recognition
→   Virtual reality (VR)

Further reading

Newkey-Burden, C. (2024) Taylor Swift. The Whole Story the Fully Updated Unauthorized Biography. London: HarperCollins.

Taylor, M. F. (2024) Taylor Swift: The Brightest Star: Fully Updated to Include Eras and Poets. Boston: New Haven Publishing.

X
(formerly known as Twitter)

By Mohammad Shayan Ahmad

X-posts? X-pressions? Xeets? What do we call posts on X (formerly known as Twitter)? For now, it's still tweets. It is so ingrained in our vernacular it feels wrong to call them anything else. But to understand today what exactly X is and how it relates to investigative journalism, we must look back at the platform before Elon Musk took over in 2022.

What is X?

X is a social networking and microblogging platform that changed the world of information and news after its initial release in 2006. The platform allows users to write posts or share pictures in a scrollable feed that other users can view. These micro-posts, originally limited to 140 characters and gradually expanded later, are still known as tweets and allow users to continuously share information with the internet in real-time.

This is the formal, or original, definition of X. The informal, more contemporary one, is that X is a platform where users should be able to enjoy complete freedom of speech, led by a self-proclaimed "free speech absolutist." [1] It is the leading social media platform to form and share your opinion with those who also share the same opinion—and those who very much don't, essentially turning it into a battleground.

Soon after its launch, Twitter became the leading platform for sharing political, entertainment and lifestyle content, as well as other forms of news. Reporters and journalists, the world over made their own Twitter accounts, so they could promote their work and reach new audiences. But as the platform grew, it became a super-spreader of misinformation and disinformation; also falling victim to swarms of bots, significantly impacting its reliability.

Despite this, X has had an undeniable impact on mainstream media and journalism over the past decade. It allowed people to keep up to date with the news minute-by-minute, as professional and citizen journalists took to the platform to share instantaneous updates. It also opened new worlds to journalists looking to cover stories of marginalized voices and communities.

The making of a giant

In 2023, 53% of adult Americans on the platform used X as a source of news. [2] As it became the preferred method of communication for politicians and celebrities alike, news channels and journalists would analyze these tweets and recognize them as official statements.

Journalists have also been able to use the platform as a treasure trove for scandal, scouring through digital footprints and holding public figures to account for past (and perhaps present) beliefs. But perhaps the full potential of Twitter to the world of journalism was truly put in the spotlight during the so-called Arab Spring. In 2011, Andy Carvin, a Twitter marketing strategist, despite being thousands of miles away from the uprisings, utilized the platform as a tool for real-time reporting and crowdsourcing journalism, leveraging his network of contacts, particularly on-the-ground activists and demonstrators, to gather and disseminate information on the protests. [3] He would tweet updates, share images and videos, and curate a diverse range of opinions and discussions about the unfolding events—later earning him awards for innovation in journalism. This completely transformed the way journalists covered stories, as now there was another channel to gather information—and the entire world could see what was happening in real-time.

The platform also became instrumental for journalists in countries where media freedom is either limited or it is physically difficult to cover stories live due to dangerous circumstances.

For years, news channels were able to gather information from the ground on Twitter and even so-called Twitter feuds, when celebrities or politicians argue publicly on the platform, became fodder for headlines. As the misinformation proliferated, however, major news channels started running unverified claims, and we went back to square one. Soon enough, these strategies and missteps led to a distrust in the stories shared on Twitter, impacting the integrity of the real-time storytelling it had become famous for.

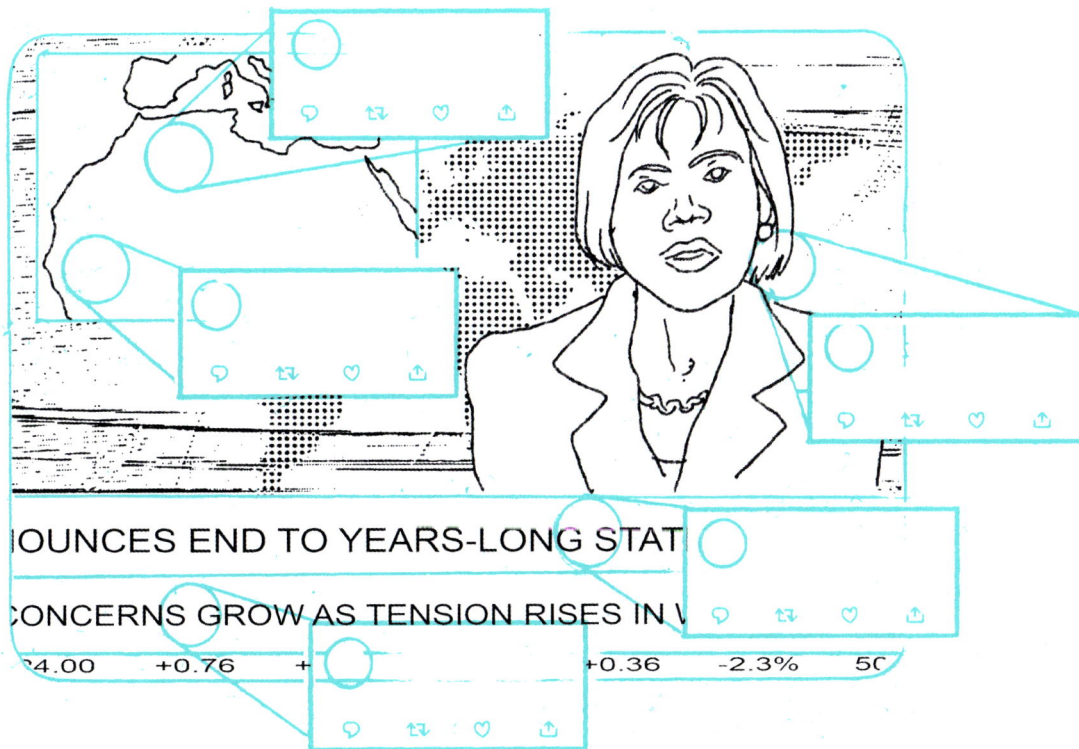

Today, Musk's plans for the platform makes us wonder what the future holds for X. Despite his stated mission to allow complete freedom of speech on the platform, the truth can be harder to find than ever. The option to buy verifications and 'blue ticks' has further exacerbated this. The ultimate form of credibility on Twitter, they hold no value on X, since anyone can buy one. Bots have also become a major issue, promoting random websites and sources that are usually phishing scams, while also being used to promote propaganda and incite narrative warfare (see page 34 for more).

The use of X—and other social media platforms, from Instagram to TikTok—in journalism is no longer a priority and while individual accounts can still be used as a source (after voracious fact checking), we can no longer, in the same way, rely on those minute-by-minute updates that once promised to turn the media universe on its head.

1 Musk, E. [ElonMusk] (2022, March 5) Starlink has been told by some governments (not Ukraine) to block Russian news sources. We will not do so unless at gunpoint. Sorry to be a free speech absolutist [Tweet]. Retrived from: x.com/elonmusk/status/1499976967105433600?s=20

2 Liedke, J & Wang, L. (Nov 1, 2023) 'Social Media and News Fact Sheet'. Retrieved from: pewresearch.org/journalism/fact-sheet/social-media-and-news-fact-sheet/#find-out-more

3 Hermida, A., Lewis, S. C., & Zamith, R. (2014) 'Sourcing the Arab Spring: A Case Study of Andy Carvin's Sources on Twitter during the Tunisian and Egyptian Revolutions', Journal of Computer-Mediated Communication, 19(3), 479–499. Retrieved from: academic.oup.com/jcmc/article/19/3/479/4067573

Related terms

→ Twitterization
→ Social media
→ Live tweeting
→ Microblogging
→ Twitter threads
→ Truth Social
→ Retweeting
→ Hashtags

Further reading

Dagoula, C. (2022) News Journalism and Twitter: Disruption, Adaptation, and Normalisation. Abingdon: Routledge.

Mezrich, B. (2023) Breaking Twitter: Elon Musk and the Most Controversial Corporate Takeover in History. New York: Grand Central.

Fore

A   B   C   D   E

F   G   H   I   J

Jais

K   L   M   N   O

Open
Source

eight

Jais

By Amal Zeyad Ali

You would think a language over 400 million people speak would be widespread online and yet only 0.5–0.6% of the top 10 million websites whose content language we know, use Arabic as of July 2024.[1] This means many Arabic speakers must be proficient in another language to navigate the internet and use AI tools such as ChatGPT, which has limited Arabic-language capabilities.[2] As you can imagine, many efforts and initiatives have been put in place to make Arabic a more accessible language, at the forefront of our lives, including Jais, which falls under the United Arab Emirates' (UAE) pioneering AI strategy.

There is only one country in the world with a Minister of State for Artificial Intelligence and that is the UAE. It was the first country in the region to adopt an AI strategy back in 2017, aiming to boost government performance in all sectors, creating a new AI market with high value. One of the most exciting elements of this initiative is Jais, a first-of-its-kind Arabic large language model (LLM) whose open-source release was announced in August 2023. Named after the UAE's highest peak, Jebel Jais, it was developed in partnership with Inception, a subsidiary of G42, an Abu Dhabi company, and Mohamed bin Zayed University of Artificial Intelligence, along with California-based private company Cerebras Systems.[3] It was trained on the Condor Galaxy 1 supercomputer on 116 billion Arabic tokens of data and 279 billion English tokens. The first model, Jais-13B, had 13 billion parameters, while the second, Jais-30B, has 30 billion.

Not only does Jais open avenues for Arabic speakers, but it could also pave the way for other underrepresented languages. Future iterations will allow for document processing, voice conversation capabilities and enterprise support with subscription models for businesses seeking customized functionalities. Currently, it allows users to seek answers, summarize information and find solutions.

But what could this mean for an investigative journalist trying to navigate hidden truths within centuries-old cultures and traditions?

While an Arabic LLM contributes to better representation and interconnectedness in our digital universe, especially for bilingual speakers, most AI language models around the world are spearheaded by private companies versus governments. The top-down approach of Jais, while unique in the field of AI, raises concerns around power, control and surveillance. Freedom in the World, a 2024 report by Freedom House that assesses political rights and civil liberties to determine a countries 'freedom' score, gave the UAE 18 (out of 100), which places the country at the lower end of the freedom index. The State of Qatar, which also launched an Arabic LLM in May 2024 called Fanar, has a score of 25, and while seven points higher than the UAE, it also places the country quite low. These lower scores spark questions regarding the freedom an AI model developed by these countries could have. Could this be the turn in the curve, or could it lead to limitations within the language model?

With the Gulf countries—such as Saudi Arabia and the UAE—spending more money globally on AI,[4] there have been questions over their use of spyware and surveillance, and whether issues such as privacy, bias and censorship can truly be resolved within a government programme. AI tools, such as ChatGPT, have become useful in journalistic investigations, but will the same become of Jais and Fanar? Are they tools for oppression or freedom? Is this a method to place these countries on the global stage, or will they merely become alternative means of surveillance? And with Jais being trained to adhere to local culture, customs and rules,[5] can it really be used to uncover truth, the fundamental pillar of journalism?

Jais is trained to understand language, but also Arabic culture and context, in that it can compute localized references and idiomatic expressions, emphasizing regionally relevant knowledge and datasets. It is a step forward in terms of Arabic-language representation, preservation and accessibility, yet its origins may be deemed unfit for journalistic investigations due to privacy concerns and safety limitations. Jais proves that while a software may seem exciting, useful and a piece in the puzzle of representation, one should also practice discretion, vigilance and triangulation, even if you are not a journalist.

1   W3Techs (2024, July 30) 'Usage statistics of Arabic for websites.' Retrieved from: w3techs.com/technologies/details/cl-ar-; DataReportal, & We Are Social, & Meltwater (2024, January 31) 'Languages most frequently used for web content as of January 2024, by share of websites' [Graph]. In Statista. Retrieved July 30, 2024, from https://www.statista.com/statistics/262946/most-common-languages-on-the-internet/

2   Look, A. (2023, October 4) 'Arabic AI could help open doors for other languages', CNN. Retrieved from: cnn.com/2023/10/04/middleeast/jais-arabic-ai-open-doors-spcintl/index.html

3   'Meet "Jais", The World's Most Advanced Arabic Large Language Model Open Sourced by G42's Inception' (2023, August 20) Mohamed bin Zayed University of Artificial Intelligence. Retrieved from: mbzuai.ac.ae/news/meet-jais-the-worlds-most-advanced-arabic-large-language-model-open-sourced-by-g42s-inception

4   Schaer, C. (2023, July 6) 'Gulf states spending big on AI: Opportunity or oppression?', DW. Retrieved from: amp.dw.com/en/gulf-states-spending-big-on-ai-opportunity-or-oppression/a-65840985

5   Look, A. (2023, October 4) 'Arabic AI could help open doors for other languages', CNN. Retrieved from: cnn.com/2023/10/04/middleeast/jais-arabic-ai-open-doors-spcintl/index.html

6   Cabral, A. R. (2023, August 30) 'Abu Dhabi-developed AI large language model for Arabic unveiled', The National. Retrieved from: thenationalnews.com/business/technology/2023/08/30/abu-dhabi-developed-ai-large-language-model-for-arabic-unveiled/

Related terms

→   Tokens
→   Parameters
→   Large language model (LLM)
→   Apache License
→   Press freedom

Open Source

By Katy Gillett

It is hard to quantify how many lives could be saved by TensorFlow, an open-source machine learning framework developed by Google Brain and released in 2015. It has been described as a library of machine learning and deep neural networks, a "toolbox for solving extremely complex mathematical problems," and it can be used for various medical applications, such as diagnosing skin cancer or analyzing MRI images for brain tumors.[1] This is only one example of how allowing AI tools to be open source has become a force for good. But what do we mean by 'open source'?

In the context of AI, 'open source' refers to software or tools for which the source code is available to the public, allowing it to be viewed, modified and distributed by anyone. It offers:

→   Transparency: Researchers and developers are better able to understand how the AI models and algorithms work, helping to verify results and prevent hidden biases or errors.

→   Collaboration: It encourages developers, researchers and organizations to work together, leading to faster advancements and innovations.

→   Customization: Users can modify tools to suit their needs, whether that's an organization with a specific requirement or someone working on niche applications.

→   Accessibility: It lowers the barrier for entry, meaning individuals and/or organizations don't need to buy expensive software licenses, allowing more people to experiment with and utilize these technologies—in turn ensuring people of all different backgrounds and social statuses infuse their own experiences into the systems.

→   Ethics and accountability: It promotes ethical AI development by enabling scrutiny and accountability, allowing for peer review, and making sure our future systems are developed responsibly.

As with anything, the concept of open source can be a double-edged sword, as it has been criticized for several reasons.[2] Key among these is the fact that open-source AI tools can be accessed by anyone, including malicious actors who might use these technologies to develop harmful applications, such as deepfakes, automated phishing attacks or to commit other cybercrimes.

There are also serious data privacy concerns, since open-source AI needs large datasets for training, which may include personal or sensitive information, leading to a risk of data breaches or misuse. Making sure these open-source tools comply with data privacy regulations such as General Data Protection Regulation can also be challenging. The lack of accountability is a concern, since the decentralized nature of open-source tools means that responsibility for ethical breaches can be unclear.

At the same time, there are issues surrounding intellectual property protection, a loss of competitive advantage and monetization in industry, cost of maintenance, quality control, community management, and forking and fragmentation, which can lead to multiple versions of a software, ultimately diluting quality, focus and resources. But there's no denying the positive impact some of these tools have had.

TensorFlow has been widely used in academic research and industry. It has been used not only to help develop AI models for medical diagnosis, but also disaster response and projects for environmental conservation, such as monitoring wildlife populations and detecting illegal deforestation through satellite imagery.[3]

1 Benbrahim, H. et al (2020, August) 'Deep Convolutional Neural Network with TensorFlow and Keras to Classify Skin Cancer Images', Scalable Computing Practice and Experience 21(3): 379-390. Retrieved from: researchgate.net/publication/343409875_Deep_Convolutional_Neural_Network_with_TensorFlow_and_Keras_to_Classify_Skin_Cancer_Images

2 Tozzi, C. (2023, November 22) '6 common problems with open source code integration', TechTarget. Retrieved from: techtarget.com/searchapparchitecture/tip/Common-problems-with-open-source-code-integration

3 White, T. (2018, March 21) 'The fight against illegal deforestation with TensorFlow', Google. Retrieved from: blog.google/technology/ai/fight-against-illegal-deforestation-tensorflow/

4 Habes, M. and Bdoor, S. (2024, March 30) 'Use Chat GPT in Media Content Production Digital Newsrooms Perspective', Artificial Intelligence in Education: The Power and Dangers of ChatGPT in the Classroom (pp. 545-561), DOI: 10.1007/978-3-031-52280-2 34.

Other examples of open-source AI projects are PyTorch, a machine learning library developed by Meta's AI Research lab, and, of course, OpenAI's GPT models, which even helped write this article (even though it may have been more of a hindrance than helpful thanks to its dodgy fact-checking capabilities). Yet this is perhaps one of the best examples of how open-source AI technology has transformed journalism.[2] While GPT-3 and GPT-4 are not open source, GPT-2 is and this is what was experimented with early on by newsrooms to automate standard content creation—such as financial earnings, sports events and weather updates—freeing up humans to focus on more in-depth reporting. While the ChatGPT models may not be used in newsrooms, similar chatbot-style platforms have been created for publications, allowing journalists to better tell data-driven stories, as well as assisting with information extraction. These models have also allowed for enhanced customization of news feeds, engaging more audiences and boosting reader retention.

Of course, the potential downsides of open-source AI tools' adoption in journalism are many. We must bear in mind how vulnerable they can be to security risks, how they can lead to data breaches and propagate the spread of misinformation. Their inherent biases could also lead to skewed or discriminatory reporting, undermining the credibility and objectivity of journalistic content. There are also questions over quality and credibility, authorship, job displacement and skills erosion.

But if these tools can quite literally save lives, can we all work together to help mitigate these downsides?

Related terms

→ Open data
→ Open access
→ Creative Commons
→ Open innovation
→ Crowdsourcing

Further reading

Eghbal, N. (2020) Working in Public: The Making and Maintenance of Open Source Software. San Francisco: Stripe Press.

Moody, G. (2001) Rebel Code: Linux and the Open Source Revolution. New York: Basic Books.

Raymond, E. S. (2001) The Cathedral & the Bazaar: Musings on Linux and Open Source by an Accidental Revolutionary. Sebastopol: O'Reilly Media.

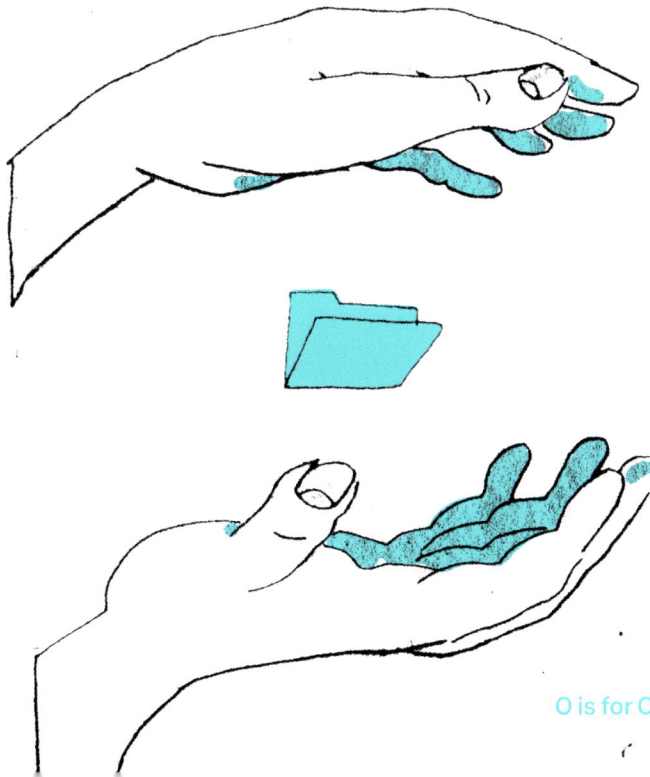

Qatar National AI Strategy

By Maryam Al-Khater

Qatar's ambitious attempts to diversify its economy through sports, education and media have now led the country to focus on technology, and in particular AI.

Qatar firmly believes in the importance of integrating rapidly developing technologies with national roots and foresight in an inspiring environment for research and innovation, given the pervasive impact of AI on all aspects of life. This commitment is articulated in Qatar's National Vision 2030, which serves as a roadmap for its transformation into an advanced nation capable of achieving sustainable development in the long term and addressing challenges while considering the needs of current and future generations. [1]

The vision identifies four pillars that are integral to AI developments: human, social, environmental and economic development. [2] The latter emphasizes a diversified knowledge-based economy focused on scientific research, high-level education, development, innovation, and the provision of physical and informational infrastructure in an open and flexible environment capable of competing in a changing world, particularly in transitioning towards an AI future. [3]

To this end, Qatar has established a general framework for developing a comprehensive national strategy according to global technological changes, with consistent sectoral strategies and implementation plans in three phases: the first National Development Strategy (2011–2016), the second (2018–2022) and the third (2024–2030). [4] The Council of Ministers also issued Decision No. 10 in 2021, establishing the AI Committee within the Ministry of Communications and Information Technology and a membership of different related governmental ministries.

Competitiveness in AI

AI excellence is deemed necessary due to the challenges posed by rapid global competitiveness in this emerging field. Qatar is no different, as its participation and development of AI tools are necessary for the nation not to lag. To achieve this goal, the Ministry of Communication and Information Technology has developed a National AI Strategy, which addresses the threats posed by AI, such as the potential job losses due to automation. [5] Conversely, it also highlights opportunities for investment to develop the capabilities of the national workforce in IT and future production means. [6]

The 2019 strategy focuses on two main areas: unleashing capabilities to produce world-class smart tools in alignment with national areas of interest and enabling production in a scientifically competent and innovation-stimulating environment under sound regulatory and ethical guidelines. [7]

The strategy revolves around six pillars aimed at transforming Qatar into an AI-centric nation in all aspects of life, business and governance, to secure its economic and strategic future. It prepares the community to embrace AI by ensuring the readiness of infrastructure for data and information investment, enhancing competitiveness in the global economy, transitioning from consumption to production, developing solutions, and achieving national and sustainable development goals. [8]

1   General Secretariat for Development Planning of Qatar (2008, July) 'Qatar National Vision 2030'. Retrieved from: psa.gov.qa/en/qnv1/Documents/QNV2030_English_v2.pdf

2   Government Communications Office, State of Qatar (n.d.) 'Qatar National Vision 2030'. Retrieved from: gco.gov.qa/en/about-qatar/national-vision2030/

3   General Secretariat for Development Planning of Qatar (2008, July) 'Qatar National Vision 2030'. Retrieved from: psa.gov.qa/en/qnv1/Documents/QNV2030_English_v2.pdf

4   Ministry of Development Planning and Statistics (2018, September) 'Qatar Second National Development Strategy 2018–2022'. Retrieved from: psa.gov.qa/en/knowledge/Documents/NDS2Final.pdf; Qatar General Secretariat for Development Planning (2011, March) 'Qatar National Development Strategy 2011–2016'. Retrieved from: psa.gov.qa/en/nds1/Documents/Downloads/NDS_EN_0.pdf; Planning and Statistics Authority, State of Qatar (n.d.) 'Third Qatar National Development Strategy 2024–2030'. Retrieved from: psa.gov.qa/en/nds1/nds3/Documents/QNDS3_EN.pdf

5   Ministry of Communications and Information Technology of Qatar, National Artificial Intelligence Strategy for Qatar, 2019. Retrieved from: mcit.gov.qa/sites/default/files/national_artificial_intelligence_strategy_for_qatar_2019.pdf https://www.mcit.gov.qa/sites/default/files/national_artificial_intelligence_strategy_for_qatar_ar.pdf

6   Ibid.

7   Ibid

8   Ibid.

9   Ibid.

The Six Pillars

These pillars begin with education and training, emphasizing the importance of specialized skills for AI development and setting priorities for integrating AI into formal education curricula. Then there is data access, which stresses the need for governance, access and sharing principles in line with Qatari laws, addressing privacy challenges and enhancing competitiveness through data exchange between Qatari institutions.

A changing workforce pillar focuses on strategic and harmonious reliance on AI to support productivity, enhance job quality and manage labor influx, while anticipating full automation in certain roles.

An emphasis on business and economic opportunities also encourages existing and new businesses to adopt AI with government support in terms of data, computing infrastructure, investment commitments and financial aids, while integrating AI into public services.

The fifth pillar identifies key areas for AI solutions, including developing generative models for Arabic-language processing (see more on page 48), national security for cyber threat analysis, precision medicine, system biology, advanced genomics, food, water, energy security, and smart agriculture and irrigation solutions. It also leverages World Cup data to improve tourism infrastructure and AI applications in the oil and gas sector to enhance efficiency and logistics. [9]

Finally, an ethics and public policy underscores Qatar's strong belief in competitive and sustainable global economic integration while developing AI under transparent data policies, clear explainability and interpretability of the decisions made by AI algorithms, data-sharing policies and individual privacy in a governance framework aligned with local laws and cultural ethics. [10]

The third National Development Strategy (2024–2030), which was launched in January 2024, focuses on digitalization through becoming global leads for digitizing government services, with up to 90% of these services becoming digital. This includes increasing data exchange among government entities and achieving sustainable economic growth to drive diversification. [11] It emphasizes developing economic clusters in IT, digital services, strategic capabilities, emerging technologies, and fostering economic uniqueness through green technology and national assets like media and creative industries. [12]

10 Ministry of Communications and Information Technology of Qatar, National Artificial Intelligence Strategy for Qatar, 2019. Retrieved from: mcit.gov.qa/sites/default/files/national_artificial_intelligence_strategy_for_qatar_2019.pdf

11 Government Communications Office, State of Qatar (2024, January 10) 'Qatar Launches Third National Development Strategy 2024-2030'. Retrieved from: gco.gov.qa/en/top-news/qatar-launches-third-national-development-strategy-2024-2030/

12 Planning and Statistics Authority, State of Qatar (n.d.) 'Third Qatar National Development Strategy 2024–2030'. Retrieved from: psa.gov.qa/en/nds1/nds3/Documents/QNDS3_EN.pdf

13 Ministry of Communications and Information Technology, Digital Agenda 2030 (2024, February 27). Retrieved from: mcit.gov.qa/sites/default/files/digital_agenda_2030_full_version_english.pdf

Journey to 2030

To achieve the goals of the third National Strategy, the Ministry of Communications and Information Technology developed the 2030 Digital Agenda, focusing on understanding and leveraging the digital era's immense technological powers, including comprehensive communication, supercomputing and integrated automation. At the Qatar Economic Forum in May 2024, the Prime Minister, Sheikh Mohammed bin Abdulrahman bin Jassim Al Thani, announced a $2.5 billion allocation for the comprehensive digital transformation program, increasing technological partnerships like the Web Summit and enhancing investments in technology, innovation and AI. The key areas of focus for the country include advanced digital infrastructure, a thriving digital economy, growing innovations, integrated government, knowledge-enriched technology, and a smart society leading the future in both public and private sectors for sustainable progress and unique economic diversity.[13]

Related terms

→ AI governance
→ AI ethics
→ Digital transformation
→ Digital infrastructure
→ Innovation ecosystem
→ Data strategy
→ Cybersecurity
→ Regulatory framework
→ AI literacy
→ Sustainable AI

Robotics

By Iqra Mazhar

From delivery robots handling our packages to self-driven cars transporting passengers around neighborhoods and autonomous vacuum cleaners sprucing up our homes, the world of robotics has drastically evolved over the years. This is the field in which robots are designed and computed to produce outputs that assist human activities.

The word 'robot' is relatively new to the English language. During the early 1920s, it was introduced to the public through a Czech play called R.U.R (Rossum's Universal Robots).[1] The play depicted robots as manufactured beings designed to serve humans, highlighting the potential and ethical dilemmas of robotic labor.

Meanwhile, the Arab world had insights into early forms of robotics during the Middle Ages. Ismail al Jazari, a scholar from Upper Mesopotamia, in an area likely located in contemporary Turkey, designed and built several automata and mechanical devices, laying the foundational principles for future robotics.[2] His works influenced designs that eventually made their way to the West and Europe, showcasing early global knowledge transfer in technology.

Today, robotics tools have been largely adopted across manufacturing and service sectors to increase productivity and economic growth. For instance, robotic arms are now ubiquitous in automotive assembly lines, where they perform precise and repetitive tasks with high efficiency. In the service sector, robots are used as customer service agents in retail stores and hotels. While robotics and automation are two distinct concepts, they are also often closely related. Robotics combines engineering and computer science to design, build and operate robots, programmable machines that can undertake tasks autonomously or semi-autonomously.

Automation, on the other hand, is a broader concept, involving software, machines or other technology to perform tasks automatically, with little to no human intervention. Automation may use robots, but also involves other automatic systems that are not necessarily physical or tangible.

Automation is particularly prevalent within journalism, as these tools assist investigative journalists, enhancing their ability to gather, analyze and present news. For example, automated data collection and analysis tools allow journalists to quickly sift through vast amounts of data to identify patterns and trends. This capability is particularly useful for breaking news and live events, where real-time reporting is required.

In terms of pure robotics, drones provide another significant advantage (see more on page 102), capturing high-quality images and videos from otherwise inaccessible angles. They can enter dangerous areas, such as disaster zones or conflict regions, ensuring the safety of journalists while providing powerful visuals for reports. The reporting of the Syrian civil war, meanwhile, has benefited from drone technology, as they have regularly been used to provide crucial footage, documenting the destruction in cities like Aleppo, where it has been too dangerous for journalists to go. These visuals support investigative reports on the impact of the conflict, offering powerful evidence and insights into the conditions on the ground.

In newsrooms, automation also aids social media posting, Natural Language Processing for transcription and translation, and fact-checking.[3] Data mining and surveillance capabilities are also invaluable for investigative journalism, enabling the uncovering of hidden information and verification of facts (see more on page 30).

As the field of robotics continues to advance, several exciting future applications are on the horizon, from healthcare to environmental monitoring and even space exploration. In healthcare, advances in precision robotics are leading to the development of surgical robots that can perform minimally invasive procedures with high accuracy. In environmental monitoring, robots equipped with sensors can monitor environmental conditions, track pollution levels, and collect data from remote or hazardous locations. Drones and robotic systems are used for wildlife monitoring and conservation efforts,

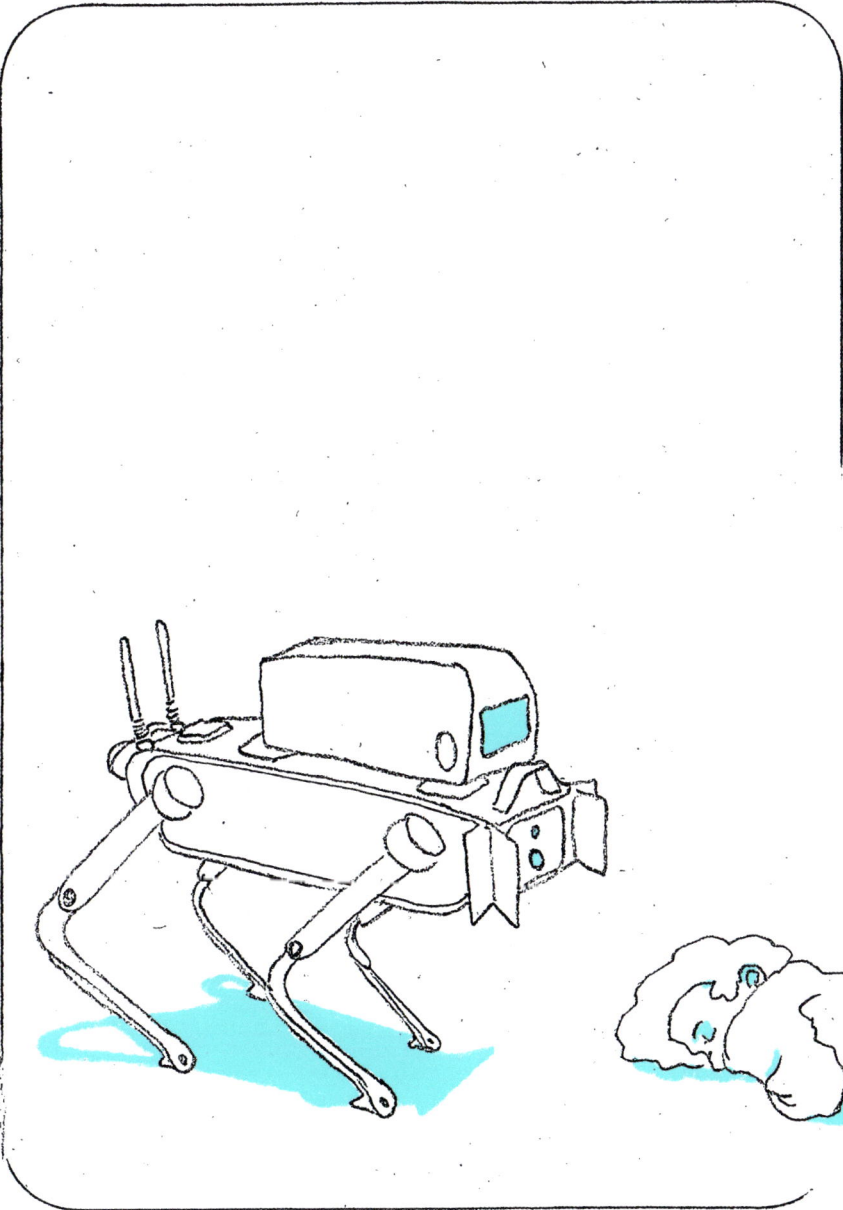

tracking animal populations and protecting endangered species. In space exploration, robotic rovers are being developed for exploration of other planets, capable of navigating harsh terrains and conducting scientific experiments, while robots are also assisting with maintenance tasks on the International Space Station, reducing the need for human spacewalks. [4]

In journalism, automation tools could further aid fact-checking systems that can cross-reference vast databases in real-time to verify the accuracy of information. Robots could assist in conducting interviews, using advanced Natural Language Processing to ask questions and analyze responses. Immersive journalism could also be revolutionized by robotic cameras that capture 360-degree footage, providing audiences with interactive,

on-the-ground experiences of news events. Autonomous drones might be used for live reporting from inaccessible areas, delivering real-time updates.

Despite the many exciting possibilities, there are just as many apprehensions surrounding the integration of robotics and automation into various industries and our lives, in particular in employment and job displacement, as robots are increasingly taking over routine and repetitive tasks in manufacturing, logistics and customer service. Biased algorithms, accountability, privacy and equitable access are also key concerns. Yet robotics continues to be integrated into our daily lives.

As the field of robotics continues to quickly evolve, we must prioritize questioning and addressing these ethical concerns, ensuring that these tools complement our lives rather than dominate. Whether in journalism, manufacturing or healthcare, robotics plays a vital role and will continue to do so for a long time to come. Future advancements, such as the integration of robotics with the Internet of Things (IoT) and advancements in AI, promise even greater potential and perhaps even greater challenges.

1   Wessling, B. (2022 January 25) '101 years ago: origins of the word "robot"', The Robot Report. Retrieved from: therobotreport.com/101-years-ago-origins-of-the-word-robot/

2   Tasci, U. N. (2020) 'Why Ismail al Jazari is called the father of medieval robots', TRTWORLD. Retrieved from: trtworld.com/magazine/why-ismail-al-jazari-is-called-the-father-of-medieval-robots-36840

3   Kuras, D. (2024, May 7) 'Top 22 AI Journalists and Reporters – The 2024 List', Prowly. Retrieved from: prowly.com/magazine/ai-journalists/

4   NASA (n.d.) 'Mobile Servicing System'. Retrieved from: nasa.gov/international-space-station/mobile-servicing-system

Related terms

→   Algorithm
→   Machine learning
→   Automation
→   Natural Language Processing (NLP)
→   Computer science

Further reading

Asimov, I. (1950) I, Robot. New York: Gnome Press.

Aylett, R. & Vargas, P.A. (2021) Living with Robots: What Every Anxious Human Needs to Know. Cambride (MA): MIT Press.

Ford, M. (2015) Rise of the Robots: Technology and the Threat of a Jobless Future. New York: Basic Books.

Ubiquitous

By Katy Gillett

Maybe you've never used ChatGPT. Maybe you don't have an Alexa running your household. Perhaps you haven't integrated any AI productivity tools into your work practice at all. But whether you know it or not, AI has permeated your life and habits in several ways.

Right now, people all over the world wake up to scroll through their smartphones, reading the morning news, which has been curated by AI-driven algorithms, personalized to their preferences. Depending on what you're reading, whether it's a sports report, a rundown on the day's stock markets or an in-depth investigative piece, chances are AI may have helped put it together. These articles are also often being fact-checked by AI systems to ensure accuracy.

This is already our present reality, and in future AI is only going to be more all-pervasive. It's not just a tool we use from time to time, but a ubiquitous presence that is truly transforming the way we live, work and consume—whether we like it or not. And there's plenty more to come.

AI's ubiquity in journalism

Ubiquitous AI refers to the widespread and seamless integration of AI into various facets of our lives, and how it influences countless interactions and decisions. Over the past few decades, its rapid evolution and integration into consumer technologies has been exponential, taking it from being something we only talk about to something we use daily.

In journalism, AI's ubiquity has become particularly evident over the past few years alone. By 2024, AI had already begun to dominate newsrooms globally, shaping everything from news gathering to content creation and distribution. [1] AI-driven tools like Natural Language Processing (NLP) and machine learning algorithms are being used to analyze vast datasets quickly, identify trends and generate news reports. Rather than taking the human touch out of journalism, however, this transformation is leading to more efficient news production processes and enabling reporters to focus on more investigative and in-depth reporting. Soon enough, it is believed it will not only support, but also collaborate with journalists. [2] For example, imagine an AI assistant that can conduct interviews, gather insights from social media trends and even suggest follow-up questions based on real-time analysis.

The proliferation of fake news has also speeded up the process of AI adoption, with systems being employed to detect and debunk false information swiftly. Tools like Google's Fact Check Explorer leverage AI to cross-reference information across multiple sources, ensuring that only verified news reaches the public.

That said, there have been rising global concerns about the use of AI in news production and the spread of misinformation, posing fresh challenges to newsrooms already struggling to engage with audiences. [3] Of course, not everyone believes the advantages of using AI in journalism outweigh the negatives. In particular, those working in the industry are concerned about the lack of accountability if AI gets it wrong, and its inability to understand ethics. The challenges of AI are discussed extensively throughout this publication, but they could be just as pervasive as the technology itself, if not kept in check. Ethical concerns around bias in AI algorithms (see page 98 for more), the potential loss of jobs due to automation, and issues of transparency and accountability are all hot topics. In business, whether journalism or another industry, greedy leaders may lean on automation and other AI advantages to reap rewards, but many experts believe true success will only come to 'organizations with soul', which lean instead on humans who care, using AI simply as a tool to facilitate efficiency. [4]

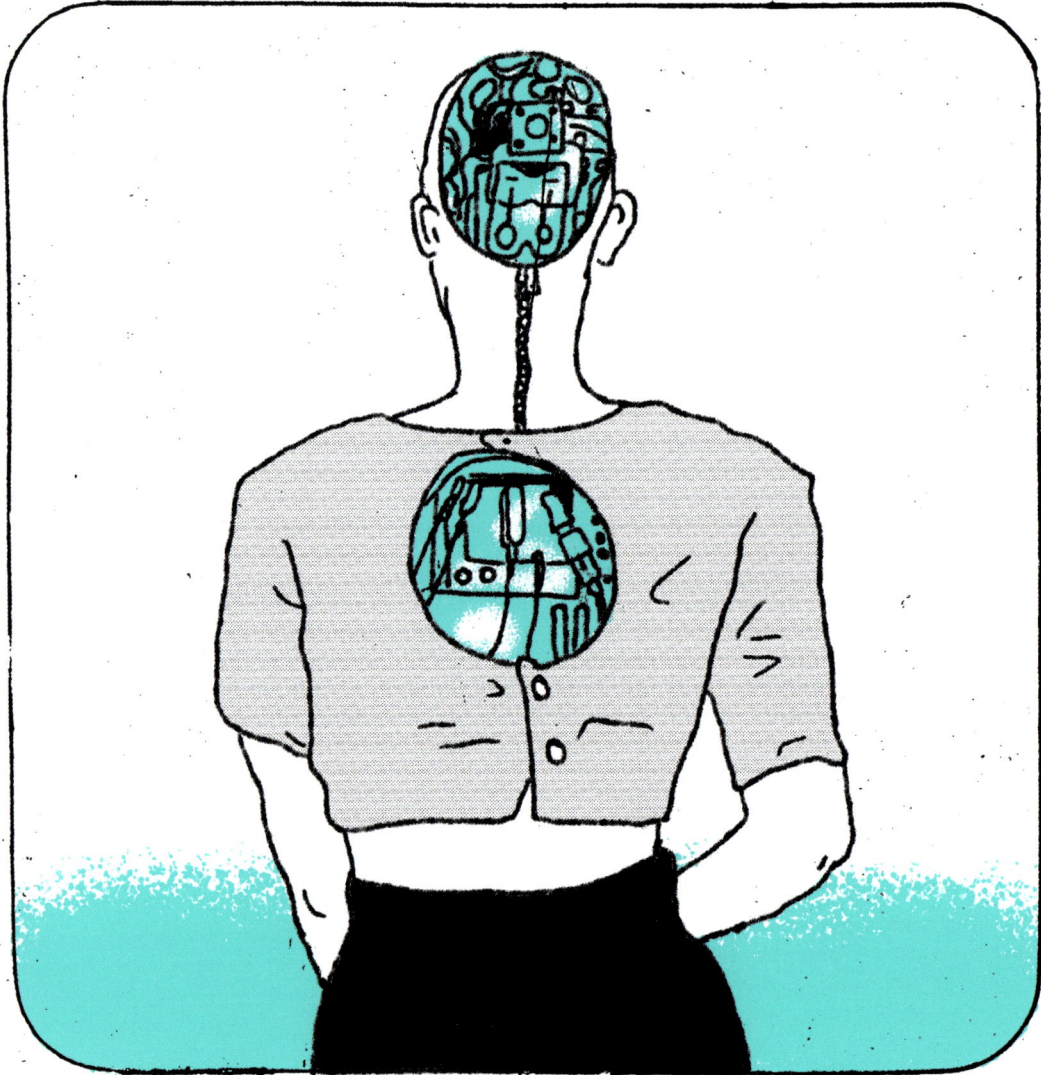

U is for Ubiquitous

1 Gupta, N. (2024, July 29) 'JournalismAI encourages newsrooms to work together in leveraging AI', World Association of News Publishers. Retrieved from: wan-ifra.org/2024/07/collaboration-key-to-leverage-ai-in-newsrooms-findings-from-journalismai/

2 Nkosi, M. (2024, November 4) 'How Are AI & Journalism Shaping the Future of News?', IT News Africa. Retrieved from: itnewsafrica.com/2024/11/how-are-ai-journalism-shaping-the-future-of-news

3 Dang, S. (2024, June 18) 'Global Audiences Suspicious of AI-Powered Newsrooms, Report Finds', Reuters. Retrieved from: reuters.com/technology/artificial-intelligence/global-audiences-suspicious-ai-powered-newsrooms-report-finds-2024-06-16

4 Marouf, L. (2023, October 9) 'In A World Of Ubiquitous AI, We Need Organizations With Soul', Forbes. Retrieved from: forbes.com/sites/forbesbooksauthors/2023/10/09/in-a-world-of-ubiquitous-ai-we-need-organizations-with-soul

Beyond the news

AI's usefulness extends far beyond the news content we consume, as it begins to interconnect every aspect of our lives, from our smart homes—where AI-powered devices like thermostats, lights and security systems adapt to user preferences and habits—to healthcare, as wearable devices and AI applications monitor our health metrics and provide personalized medical advice. On the streets, autonomous vehicles and intelligent traffic management systems are getting smarter all the time. At work, AI tools assist with productivity, communication, inventory management and decision making.

During our leisure time, more and more we see AI-driven customer service and personalized shopping experiences. For the moment, we can mostly choose whether we want to engage with these technologies. Whether or not they will eventually become all pervasive in all our lives no matter what we decide, remains to be seen.

Yet, whether you realize it or not, AI has already penetrated our lives to such an extent that you'd probably struggle to live without it in some capacity. Now it's up to you to embrace—or reject—the changes that are yet to come.

Related terms

→ Ambient intelligence
→ Internet of Things
→ Pervasive computing
→ Smart environments
→ Context-aware computing
→ Machine learning
→ Human-computer interaction

Further reading

Kissinger, H. A., et al. (2022) The Age of AI: And Our Human Future. London: John Murray.

Kurzweil, R. (2024) The Singularity Is Nearer: When We Merge with AI. New York: Viking.

Shane, J. (2019) You Look Like a Thing and I Love You: How Artificial Intelligence Works and Why It's Making the World a Weirder Place. New York: Voracious.

Yottabyte

By Mohammed Al-Sulaiti

Imagine it's 2050, and AI holds the power to capture the memory of every tweet, post, article and reel throughout history. Consider the monumental storage needed for these digital memories. This breakthrough was made possible by the emergence of the yottabyte. Just as your height in meters and weight in kilograms quantify physical attributes, a yottabyte measures a vast expanse of data, marking a new era where the limits of big data are ever-expanding.

A yottabyte is a unit measuring digital information storage, equivalent to one septillion (10^{24}) bytes. It represents an enormous data capacity, far beyond current practical use, and symbolizes the future potential of data storage. The concept has become increasingly prominent in the early twenty-first century as data creation soared due to advancements in digital technology, social media and the internet. As global digital footprints expanded, the need for massive storage capacities became critical, with storage technologies eventually evolving towards the theoretical yottabyte.

Now, the term 'yottabyte' is transforming from theoretical to practical, impacting data storage and utilization. Initially, it symbolized an immense, conceptual data scale, but technological strides have progressed from gigabytes to petabytes and exabytes.[1] Yottabytes now signify ultimate data capabilities for complex simulations, AI and comprehensive analytics.

A global divide

In the Global South, digital infrastructure was initially limited. However, the rapid adoption of mobile technology bridged the digital divide. The spread of affordable smartphones and increased internet access created vast amounts of data, underscoring the importance of large-scale storage solutions. This empowered local investigative journalists to use big data to expose corruption, human rights abuses and social justice issues. In the Arab world, the digital age, especially after the Arab Spring, saw a rise in online activism, social media usage and digital content creation. Investigative journalism increasingly relied on large data sets to uncover truths and advocate for reforms. The ability to store and analyze data on a yottabyte scale would revolutionize investigative journalism, offering unprecedented insights into governance, social dynamics and historical narratives.

The yottabyte's significance in investigative journalism lies in its potential to store and analyze vast quantities of data from various sources—tweets, articles, videos—over time. By using AI and massive data storage, journalists can uncover intricate patterns and connections, leading to more profound and impactful stories. This ability transforms the field, providing a more comprehensive understanding of events and trends across different periods and regions.

From idea to reality

The concept of a yottabyte is no longer just theoretical. Real-world applications have shown multiple entities pushing the boundaries of data storage and utilization, especially in journalism. For instance, the Human Genome Project generated petabytes of data while mapping the entire human genome. The capacity of a yottabyte would exponentially expand the scope of such projects, enabling more complex data analysis and storage.

Tech giants like Apple, Microsoft, Google and Meta manage immense amounts of data daily. Although they haven't reached yottabyte scales, their current capabilities suggest this level of data management is on the horizon.

Investigative journalism collaborations, such as the Panama Papers (see page 88 for more), have also involved vast data sets requiring sophisticated storage and analysis, hinting at the future need for yottabyte-scale storage.

However, the move towards yottabyte storage raises several controversies. Ethical issues, for one, come to the forefront, as the ability to store yottabytes of data intensifies concerns about privacy and surveillance. Journalists must navigate the ethical implications of managing such massive amounts of personal data, and protecting these large volumes from breaches and unauthorized access presents a significant security challenge.

Additionally, the advent of yottabyte storage could exacerbate the digital divide. Not all regions have equal access to advanced digital storage technologies, potentially widening the gap between developed and developing areas. With regards to climate change, this progress is also linked to and will likely increase emissions resulting from enormous demands of yottabyte-scale data centers. [2]

A wealth of benefits

While true yottabyte storage is not yet in use, extrapolating from petabyte and exabyte systems reveals several benefits. For example, the capacity allows for deeper data analysis, uncovering patterns otherwise invisible. This is particularly crucial for investigative journalism to reveal corruption, trends and systemic issues. Large datasets from diverse sources, such as social media and official records, can be analyzed together, enriching the contextual depth of reports. This aggregation of resources provides a more comprehensive understanding of complex issues, enhancing the quality and depth of journalistic investigations.

Real-world yottabyte storage could democratize data access, benefiting smaller entities and independent journalists. It enables advanced AI with deep learning models, enhancing Natural Language Processing and real-time decision-making in healthcare and autonomous vehicles. Additionally, it fosters global transparency and accountability in governance, highlighting systemic issues.

By 2050, as yottabyte storage becomes commonplace, the technological strides we initiate in 2025 will enable in-depth analyses, advanced AI models and comprehensive data access, shaping a future where information is more democratized and accessible, providing invaluable resources for the next generation of journalists, scholars and innovators.

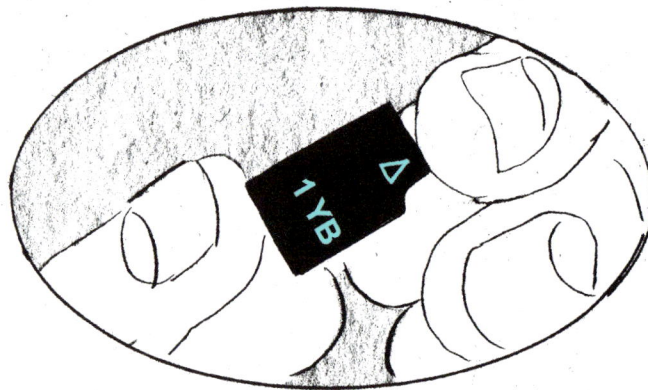

1 Matsuoka, S. et al. (2014) 'Extreme Big Data (EBD): Next generation big data infrastructure technologies towards yottabyte/year', _Supercomputing frontiers and innovations_ 1, no. 2, 89–107.

2 Mangal, P. & Rajesh, A. (2020) 'Addressing climate change-making the case for big data-based decision making framework', _International Journal of Public Sector Performance Management_, vol. 6, no. 2, 205–216.

Related terms

→ Storage capacity
→ Data center
→ Kilobyte
→ Megabyte

Further reading

Hu, F. (2016) _Big Data: Storage, Sharing, and Security_.
Boca Raton: CRC Press.

Freeman, L. (2017) _The History of Data Storage: From Cathode Ray Tubes to Resistive Ram_. Independently published.

Mayer-Schönberger, V. & Cukier, K. (2013) _Big Data: A Revolution That Will Transform How We Live, Work, and Think_.
Boston: Houghton Mifflin Harcourt.

By Ali Al Kubaisi

Have you ever started counting and said zero, one, two, three? Probably not. It seems like such an irrelevant number, holding no value. However, zero could be the missed opportunity we've been seeking for centuries.

Zero, the number representing nothingness, has had a turbulent journey through history, marked by controversy and cultural resistance. [1] The ancient Greeks, despite their profound contributions to mathematics and philosophy, couldn't comprehend the concept of zero and nothingness. For nearly 1,500 years, the number was considered taboo. In stark contrast, civilizations in what we call the Global South today, such as the Indians and Babylonians, embraced zero and integrated it into their numeral systems. [2]

The concept of infinite

The concept of zero as a number first appeared in Mesopotamia (present-day Iraq) around the third century BCE. Babylonian mathematicians used a placeholder symbol in their cuneiform script. [3] This early form of zero was crucial for maintaining the correct place value in their calculations, although it was not yet a number in its own right.

The journey of zero continued in ancient India. In his seminal work, Brāhmasphuṭasiddhānta, the Indian mathematician Brahmagupta in the seventh century CE established rules for zero, treating it as a number that could be manipulated in arithmetic operations. [4] He defined zero's behavior in addition, subtraction and multiplication, and introduced the concept of division by zero, although his interpretation of it differed from the modern understanding.

The concept spread to the Islamic world, where scholars further developed it. The work of Arab mathematician Al-Khwarizmi (see page 84 for more), for example, including his book Kitab al-Jabr wa-l-Muqabala (The Book of Restoration and Balancing), introduced the Hindu-Arabic numeral system, including zero, to the Western world. [5] While the adoption of zero in Europe was met with resistance, by the twelfth century it had become an integral part of its mathematical framework, thanks in part to Italian mathematician Leonardo Fibonacci. In his book Liber Abaci, Fibonacci promoted the use of the Hindu-Arabic numeral system, highlighting its efficiency compared to traditional Roman numerals. Ultimately, the inclusion of zero revolutionized Western science and mathematics, enabling the development of algebra, calculus and the concept of the infinite, paving the way for advancements in various fields, including, of course, modern AI.

The significance of nothingness

Today, in the realm of AI, zero holds significant relevance. Zero is crucial in binary code, the fundamental language of computers, where it represents the absence of a signal. The binary system forms the backbone of all digital computing, including AI. However, the binary nature of zero can sometimes lead to oversimplification, ignoring the complexities and nuances of real-world scenarios. For instance, in sentiment analysis, labeling a statement as positive (1) or negative (0) might miss the subtleties of human emotions and intentions. This binary approach can be problematic because it oversimplifies the complexity of human sentiment. By treating sentiment analysis as a black box and a one-size-fits-all solution, researchers risk overlooking these subtleties, leading to inaccurate or misleading results, and reducing the effectiveness of AI systems in understanding and responding to human communication. [6]

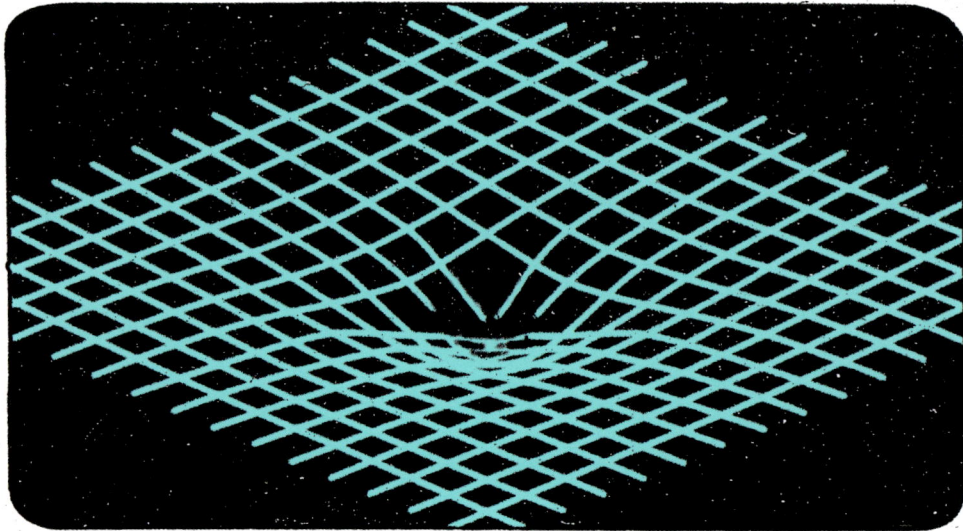

If zero were not part of our vocabulary, however, we would lose a powerful concept for conceptualizing both absence and potential. Alternatives like 'null' or 'void' might not carry the same impactful connotations of nothingness that zero does. Therefore, the implications of zero in AI are profound; it forces us to confront the unseen and unaccounted for, pushing for greater transparency and accuracy in AI systems.

Potential in the void

Looking ahead, the concept of zero in AI may evolve to encompass new dimensions of technological advancement. As quantum computing progresses, the binary system of zeros and ones may expand to include quantum states, fundamentally altering how we understand and apply zero in AI. In classical computing, a bit is either 0 or 1. A qubit, however, can be in a state of 0, 1 or any quantum superposition of these states. This ability to be in multiple states at once will dramatically increase computational potential as we know it today.

While the future holds optimistic uses for AI, it also presents moral dilemmas. Striving for absolute accuracy, like pursuing zero error rates in AI models, can sometimes result in overfitting. This occurs when models perform extraordinarily well on training data but fail in real-world applications, causing AI hallucinations (see page 106 for more). Such failures have major repercussions, particularly in critical fields like autonomous driving or medical diagnostics, where errors can be fatal.

Zero is far from an irrelevant number. It is a metaphor for possibility in the void, as well as a critical concept in the development of AI. As we navigate the myriad challenges of the modern world, the concept of zero will remain unchanged. It is through the simplicity of zero that complexity will emerge.

1   Matson, J (2009, August 21) 'The Origin of Zero', <u>Scientific American</u>. Retrieved from: scientificamerican.com/article/history-of-zero

2   Ibid.

3   Ibid.

4   Kurbalija, J. (2023, March 5) 'Origins of Zero: A fascinating story of science and spirituality across civilisations', <u>Diplo</u>. Retrieved from: diplomacy.edu/blog/origins-of-zero-a-fascinating-story-of-science-and-spirituality-across-civilisations

5   Ibid.

6   Boghe, K. (2020, July 22) 'We Need to Talk About Sentiment Analysis', <u>Medium</u>. Retrieved from: medium.com/swlh/we-need-to-talk-about-sentiment-analysis-9d1f20f2ebfb

Related terms

→   Cuneiform
→   Binary code
→   Quantum computing
→   Overfitting
→   Qubit

Further reading

Kaplan, R. (1999). <u>The Nothing That Is: A Natural History of Zero</u>.
New York: Oxford University Press.

Seife, C. (2000) <u>Zero: The Biography of a Dangerous Idea</u>.
New York: Penguin Books.

Enigma

Forensic
Architecture

Muhammad
ibn Musa
al-Khwarizmi

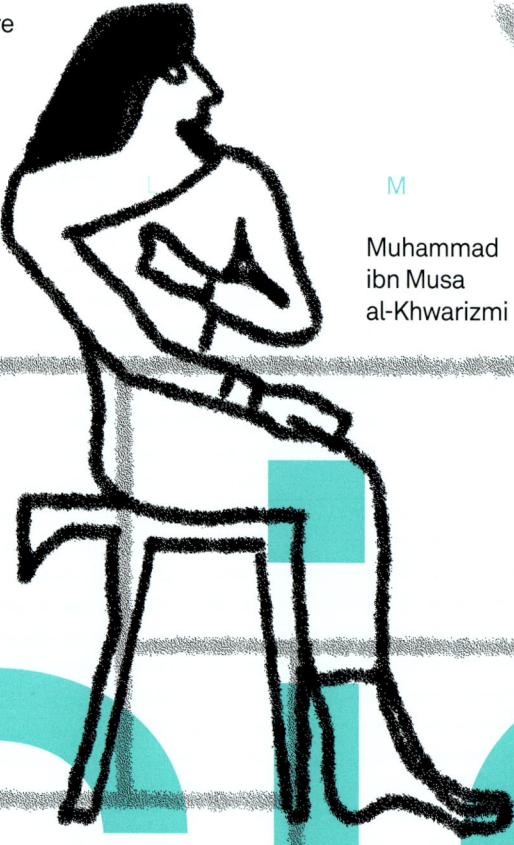

sign

sight

Papers

Whistleblower

Enigma

By Syed Mehdi

Picture a machine so complex that it baffled the brightest minds of its time. This was the Enigma, a cryptography and engineering marvel used by Nazi Germany to encrypt their most sensitive communications. The Enigma machine offered more than 150 quintillion (150,000,000,000,000,000,000) possible combinations, a number so large it is about 1.5 billion times the number of stars in the Milky Way galaxy. [1] This complexity protected Nazi communications for a significant part of World War II, posing a formidable challenge to Allied forces.

The Enigma was initially invented for commercial encryption purposes by German engineer Arthur Scherbius in 1918. [2] It was later adapted by the German military for use in World War II. It operated on the principle of a substitution cipher, utilizing a combination of rotating disks (rotors) and a plugboard to scramble plaintext messages into ciphertext. Its main components included: [3]

1   Keyboard (input): Pressing a key on the keyboard completed an electrical circuit, sending a current through the machine.

2   Rotors: The current passed through a series of rotors, each with internal wiring that mapped each letter of the alphabet to a different letter. After each key press, the rotors would rotate, changing the mapping and thereby increasing the complexity of the encryption.

3   Reflector: Upon passing through the rotors, the current reached a reflector, which redirected it back through the rotors along a different path. This ensured the encryption was symmetric, meaning the same settings could be used for both encryption and decryption.

4   Plugboard: Before and after passing through the rotors, the current went through a plugboard where pairs of letters could be swapped, adding another layer of complexity to the encryption.

5   Lampboard (output): Finally, the current lit up a lamp on the lampboard, indicating the encrypted letter.

To decrypt a message, the recipient needed to set the Enigma machine with the same rotor order and plugboard settings as used by the sender. This alignment allowed the encrypted message to be converted back into its original plaintext form.

In 1939, British mathematician Alan Turing and his team at Bletchley Park developed the Bombe, an electromechanical device, to rapidly test numerous rotor settings and crack the Enigma code. [4] The Bombe was inspired by a device called the 'bomba' from Poland and worked by simulating the Enigma's encryption process to identify settings that could produce meaningful text.

Turing and his colleagues began their work by analyzing intercepted messages for common phrases and predictable patterns, such as weather reports, salutations and repeated daily phrases. These known phrases, called 'cribs,' were crucial in deducing the rotor and plugboard settings for each day. Once a potential setting was identified, the Bombe ran through possible configurations, eliminating incorrect ones based on logical deductions until the correct settings were found. Turing also developed statistical methods and algorithms to improve the efficiency of this process, significantly reducing the number of possible settings that needed to be tested. This systematic and mathematical approach enabled the team to decrypt German communications swiftly and accurately, providing vital intelligence that greatly aided the Allied war effort. [5]

Turing's work on the Enigma machine not only revolutionized cryptography but also laid the groundwork for modern computing and AI. The methods and algorithms developed to break the Enigma code are considered early examples of AI, where machines were used to perform complex calculations and pattern recognition tasks that were beyond human capability.

The science of cryptography continues to evolve, especially as technology advances and new forms of encryption emerge. Future possibilities include the development of quantum cryptography, which could create encryption methods even more secure than those based on current technology. However, just as the Enigma was eventually cracked, future encryption systems will also face the ingenuity of those determined to break them.

Today, AI plays a crucial role in both encryption and decryption processes. Advanced AI algorithms can enhance the security of cryptographic systems by identifying vulnerabilities and predicting potential threats. At the same time, AI is used by cybersecurity experts to develop new ways to protect data from increasingly sophisticated attacks. This ongoing battle between encryption and decryption, now fueled by AI advancements, will likely continue to shape the field of cybersecurity, driving the development of more robust and secure systems.

As for Alan Turing, while his legacy did not fully come to light until long after his death—the work at Bletchley Park and Turing's role in cracking the Enigma code was not known until the 1990s—today it is widely acknowledged that his and his fellow codebreakers' efforts shortened the war by several years and saved countless lives. This story has even been immortalized in the 2014 Oscar-nominated film The Imitation Game, starring Benedict Cumberbatch. Now millions of people understand how Turing's work transcends historical boundaries, influencing contemporary practices in encryption and cybersecurity, which are critical in today's digital age.

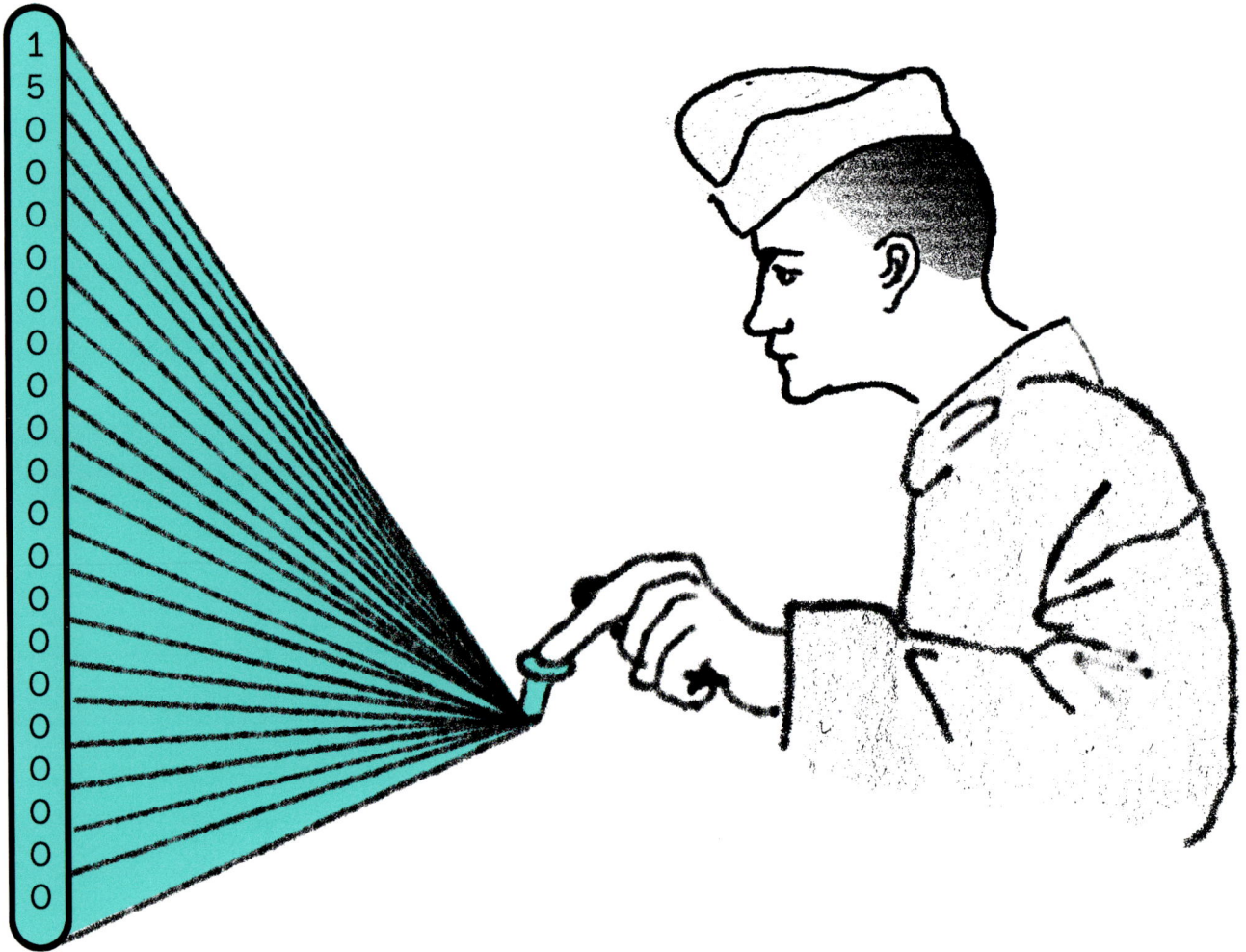

E is for Enigma

1   NASA (2015, December) 'Imagine the universe!'. Retrieved from: imagine.gsfc.nasa.gov/science/objects/milkyway1.html

2   National Cryptologic Museum (2023, January 25) no title, US Department of Defense. Retrieved from: media.defense.gov/2023/Jan/25/2003149564/-1/-1/0/NCMARTIFACTCATALOGUE.PDF

3   Hern, A. (2014, November 14) 'How did the Enigma machine work?', The Guardian. Retrieved from: theguardian.com/technology/2014/nov/14/how-did-enigma-machine-work-imitation-game

4   Raikar, S. P. (n.d.) 'Bombe', Britannica. Retrieved from: britannica.com/topic/Bombe

5   Castellano, L. C., & Peñafiel, J. (2023, July 19) 'Encryption, 80 years after the Enigma machine', El País. Retrieved from: english.elpais.com/science-tech/2023-07-19/encryption-80-years-after-the-enigma-machine.html

Related terms

→   Cryptography
→   Codebreaking
→   Cybersecurity
→   Encryption
→   Information security

Further reading

Hodges, A. (1983) Alan Turing: The Enigma.
London: Burnett Books.

Sebag-Montefiore, H. (2000) Enigma: The Battle for the Code.
New York: John Wiley & Sons.

Welchman, G. (1982) The Hut Six Story: Breaking the Enigma Codes.
London: McGraw-Hill.

Forensic Architecture

By Jack Thomas Taylor

Early in 2024, after six-year-old Palestinian child Hind Rajab was found dead in Gaza City, multidisciplinary research group Forensic Architecture was commissioned by Qatar-based news network Al Jazeera to examine the circumstances surrounding the killing of Hind, her four cousins, her aunt, uncle and the two paramedics who came to her rescue. The team were able to piece together what happened using AI-powered 3D modelling, audio analysis, geolocation and image-data complexes, while working closely with journalists from Al Jazeera's Fault Lines and Earshot, the first non-profit producing audio investigations for human rights and environmental advocacy. [1] It concluded that an Israeli tank fired at the family car from meters away, disproving previous claims by the Israeli military that its forces were not present in the area.

Without investigations such as these, much could be lost to the so-called 'fog of war'. This is exactly what Forensic Architecture is all about—uncovering hidden truths behind human rights violations, state violence and environmental crimes. [2]

How do they do it?

The group, based at Goldsmiths, University of London, is led by architect Eyal Weizman, utilizing architectural techniques and AI to investigate and present evidence in legal and political forums, making significant contributions to justice and accountability worldwide.

The team combines various disciplines, including architecture, digital modeling, journalism and human rights advocacy, to reconstruct and analyze events that are often obscured by state or corporate interests. The term 'forensic' refers to the application of scientific methods and techniques to their investigations, while 'architecture' denotes the spatial and visual analysis of these events. [3]

They use:

→ Spatial analysis: The use of architectural principles to understand the physical spaces where incidents occur, helping to reconstruct events.

→ AI-powered digital modeling: The creation of 3D models and simulations using AI to visualize and analyze the evidence.

→ Interdisciplinary collaboration: Combining expertise from various fields to create comprehensive investigations.

→ Transparency and accountability: Making their findings publicly available to promote transparency and support legal and human rights efforts.

Where they make a difference

Since its inception in 2010, Forensic Architecture has been involved in numerous high-profile investigations and their work has been presented in international courts, parliamentary inquiries and human rights reports. [4] They've worked with political institutions, climate organizations and much of their most important work is also self-initiated.

They have also helped victims tell their stories to the public in a more dynamic manner. A recent example is Situated Testimonies of Grenfell, a feature-length film created after Forensic Architecture was approached by 11 individuals—bereaved family members, survivors and nearby residents—affected by the Grenfell Tower tragedy in London, where a fire broke out in a 24-storey apartment block in North Kensington, causing 72 deaths. [5] The collaboration used an interviewing technique developed by Forensic Architecture called situated testimony, in this

1   'Israeli tank fired at Hind Rajab family car from metres away: Investigation' (2024, June 23) Al Jazeera. Retrieved from: aljazeera.com/news/2024/6/23/israeli-tank-fired-at-hind-rajab-family-car-from-metres-away-investigation

2   Forensic Architecture: About. Retrieved from: forensic-architecture.org/about/agency

3   Ibid.

4   Ibid.

case involving the use of 3D models of Grenfell Tower and its surrounding environment to help survivors and witnesses access their memories of the night of the fire, in a safe environment. These reconstructions were then pieced together with the team's own analysis, and video and audio data, to create a film that presents a shared story of that tragic night.

In journalism, Forensic Architecture's collaborations with news organizations has led to groundbreaking reports that blend rigorous analysis, bolstered by AI, with compelling storytelling. Like in the case of little Hind, whose story gained traction once more after the investigation was released.

They also look back in time, uncovering and rediscovering hidden histories. For example, the collective has been working with Nama and Ovaherero leadership groups in Namibia since 2022 to examine sites related to the 1904–1908 genocide perpetrated by the German colonial army. [6] In particular, the legacy of Shark Island, the site of the deadliest concentration camp. Through a combination of oral history with digital spatial analysis and archival research, Forensic Architecture was able to create the most comprehensive reconstruction of the camp's layout and operation to date, even identifying burial sites.

Bad actors thwart truths

While their work is widely acclaimed, it is not without its challenges and controversies. [7] The group often deals with sensitive and politically charged cases, which can lead to backlash and attempts to discredit their findings, while the reliance on AI often introduces questions about accuracy and interpretation. That is why ensuring the integrity and reliability of their reconstructions is paramount, as any inaccuracies could undermine their credibility and the legal processes they support.

The more technology progresses, the more groups like Forensic Architecture can push the boundaries of what is possible to uncover. Advances in AI, such as machine learning and computer vision, hold the potential to further enhance their investigative capabilities, improving accuracy and speed of analyses, but also making it easier to unearth and present evidence.

As global awareness of state and corporate misconduct increases, the demand for independent and reliable investigations will only grow, and so the significance of Forensic Architecture's work to date cannot be overstated. By applying architectural principles and AI technologies to forensic investigations, the group offers a powerful tool for presenting evidence of wrongdoing. Who knows how many instances of state and corporate violence might remain hidden or misunderstood if groups like Forensic Architecture ceased to exist.

5   Forensic Architecture (2024, June 4) 'The Grenfell Tower Fire: Situated Testimonies'. Retrieved from: forensic-architecture.org/investigation/the-grenfell-tower-fire-situated-testimonies

6   Forensic Architecture (2024, April 12) 'German Colonial Genocide in Namibia: The Hornkranz Massacre'. Retrieved from: forensic-architecture.org/investigation/german-colonial-genocide-in-namibia-the-hornkranz-massacre

7   Watlington, E. (2023, March 15) 'When Does Artistic Research Become Fake News? Forensic Architecture Keeps Dodging the Question', Art News. Retrieved from: artnews.com/art-in-america/features/forensic-architecture-fake-news-1234661013/

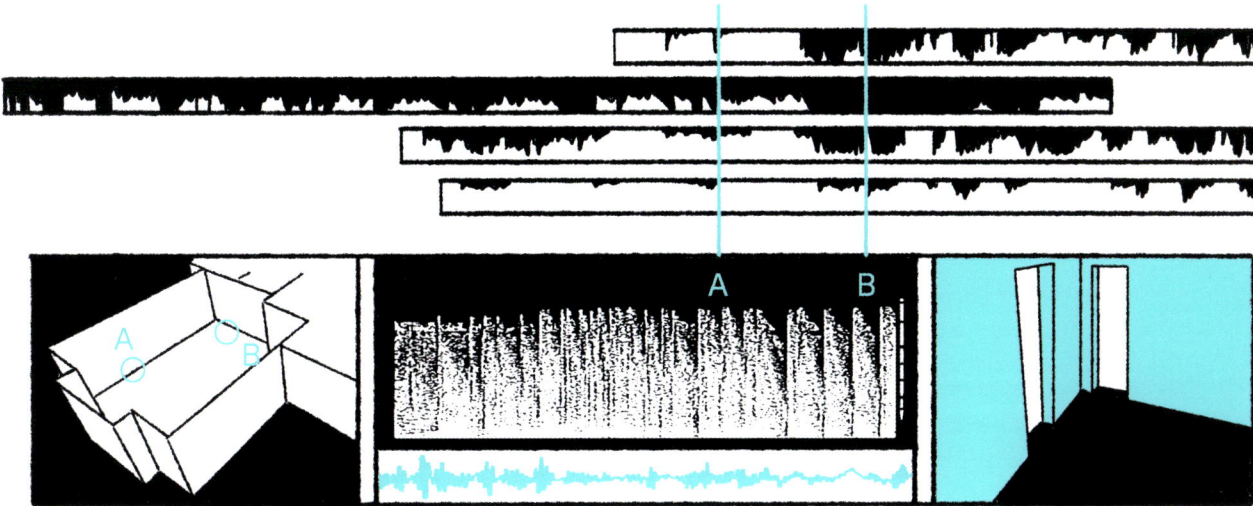

Related terms

→   Digital forensics
›   Machine learning
→   Computer vision
→   Human rights advocacy
→   Data visualization

Further reading

Weizman, E. & Fuller, M. (2001) Investigative Aesthetics: Conflicts and Commons in the Politics of Truth. London: Verso.

Weizman, E. (2017) Forensic Architecture: Violence at the Threshold of Detectability. New York: Zone Books.

Weizman, E. (2011) The Least of All Possible Evils: A Short History of Humanitarian Violence. London: Verso.

Weizman, E. (2012) Hollow Land: Israel's Architecture of Occupation. London: Verso.

Muhammad ibn Musa al-Khwarizmi

By Hind Al Saad

What connects the algorithm that influences the media we consume daily, with the algebra we studied in school, to the numerical system we use every day? They all trace back to Muhammad ibn Musa al-Khwarizmi, a Muslim Persian scholar born in the eighth century. He is one of the great scholars from the Islamic Golden Age, and he significantly contributed to the development of algebra and arithmetic—which influenced the systems we use today. This included transforming the Babylonian and Hindu numeral systems into a simple system accessible for almost anyone to use. [1]

Al-Khwarizmi is best known as the father of algebra, as he invented the method. Algebra comes from the Arabic word al-jabr, which can translate to rejoining or completion, and was part of his calculation method of moving the subtracted value to the other side of the equation. His new way of calculating and using numbers was an important discovery within the field as it was the "first and greatest step in detaching the source of mathematics from the physical and moving it into the purely abstract." [2] Up to that point, mathematics was based on geometry from the Greeks, which revolved around understanding spaces and the tangible world. Al-Khwarizmi's insights paved the way for contemporary uses of his system that aided building skyscrapers, charting planetary orbits, calculating and tracking economies, and is the basis of computational systems that drive the operation of software, algorithms and modern AI. Even though the word algorithm came directly from the Latinization of his last name, Al-Khwarizmi is often forgotten and not credited for his contribution to knowledge and technology.

An algorithm technically refers to the set of rules or steps a computer follows to solve an operation (see page 18 for more). Within internet culture today, it has become one of the central elements of social media and has taken on a more elusive meaning. At times, it's praised for how well it curates and tailors the content in our feeds to our interests, and how well it knows us. Sometimes, it alarms us by surveilling our conversations and feeding us ads and posts of things we mentioned out loud. Even though algorithms have become central agents in shaping our online experiences and what media and news we consume—influencing what we see first, what we see more of and what is censored from us—how algorithms work and the biases that are inherently embedded within the system aren't common knowledge to users.

Humans create the rules within algorithms. While the algorithms are generated through AI, the datasets are still biased, as they are based on sources created and written by humans. The dataset selection is collected and annotated by humans, and their inherent biases and judgments get transferred to the system of rules within the algorithm. People can become more aware of what influences their media consumption by demystifying these technological terms and processes, allowing the public to regain control and understanding of their online experience. This applies to journalists as well, as algorithms guide their feeds and search engines, and by understanding its process, they can find different ways to break through the algorithm and the censorship to find the sources and facts.

There is a vast disconnect between the algorithm's word origin and its application today—from Al-Khwarizmi's moral values that motivated his pursuit of knowledge and the resulting discoveries to the capitalistic use of algorithms now. Al-Khwarizmi was interested in creating valuable methods to ease everyday needs, as he conveyed in his book: "What is easiest and most useful in arithmetic, such as men constantly require in cases of inheritance, legacies, partition, lawsuits, and trade, and in all their dealings with one another, or where the measuring of lands, the digging of canals, geometrical computations, and other objects of various sorts and kinds are concerned." [3]

As Islam was the shared value between the scholars at the time, they were motivated by its branching values: knowledge (<u>ilm</u>), trusteeship (<u>khilafa</u>), justice (<u>adl</u>) and public interest (<u>istislah</u>). ▪ In present times, the guiding force of industries is capitalism. Public interest is no longer at the forefront of the development of knowledge and technologies. This shift in values leads to algorithms that influence our online experiences—skewing what we consume to control narratives and perceptions, and creating an experience based on increasing engagement and screen time, making it harder for public interest and justice to prevail.

1. Turner, H. R. (1999) Science in Medieval Islam: An illustrated introduction. Austin, University of Texas Press.

2. Morgan, M. H. (2007) Lost History: The Enduring Legacy of Muslim Scientists, Thinkers, and Artists. Washington, D.C.: National Geographic.

3. Ibid.

4. Sardar, Z. (2006) How Do You Know: Reading Ziauddin Sardar on Islam, Science and Cultural Relations. London: Pluto Press, 146–148.

Related terms

→ Algebra
→ Algorithm
→ Arithmetic
→ Numerals
→ Mathematics
→ Islamic Golden Age

Further reading

Morgan, M. H. (2007) Lost History: The Enduring Legacy of Muslim Scientists, Thinkers, and Artists. Washington, D.C.: National Geographic.

Turner, H. R. (1997) Science in Medieval Islam: An illustrated introduction. Austin: University of Texas Press.

Papers

By Katy Gillett

Nowhere has AI perhaps proved more useful in journalism so far than in investigations exposing the shadowy financial dealings of the world's elite. This intersection of modern technology and human creativity has birthed monumental exposés such as the Panama Papers, Paradise Papers and Pandora Papers.

In 2016, the Panama Papers unveiled offshore financial dealings and tax avoidance schemes orchestrated by a Panamanian law firm, Mossack Fonseca. [1] The leak encompassed 11.5 million documents spanning almost four decades and detailing the hidden fortunes of politicians, celebrities and business leaders all over the world. The records were given by an anonymous source to the German newspaper Süddeutsche Zeitung, which shared them with the Washington DC-based non-profit International Consortium of Investigative Journalists, which in turn passed them on to a large network of international partners, including the BBC and The Guardian. The investigation exposed a web of offshore entities that were being used to evade taxes, launder money and circumvent international sanctions, implicating public figures such as Pakistan's former Prime Minister Nawaz Sharif, Iceland's former Prime Minister Sigmundur Davíð Gunnlaugsson and Sergei Roldugin, reported by many sources as one of the closest friends of Russian President Vladimir Putin.

The following year came the Paradise Papers, which continued the saga, revealing similar activities involving Appleby, a Bermuda-based law firm, further exposing misuse of offshore tax havens. [2] This entailed a cache of 13.4 million documents, again leaked to reporters at Süddeutsche Zeitung, which detailed the financial affairs of multinational corporations such as Nike and Apple, as well as high-profile individuals like Queen Elizabeth II and US Commerce Secretary Wilbur Ross. For the first time, certain methods employed by the global elite to exploit loopholes in international tax regulations were publicly exposed.

In a hat trick for journalism, the Pandora Papers then came in 2021, unveiling even more secrets of global elites hiding wealth offshore. [3] This was the biggest leak yet, consisting of 11.9 million documents from 14 different offshore service providers in countries such as Panama, Switzerland and the UAE, revealing the financial machinations of more than 330 politicians and public officials from over 90 countries, including former British Prime Minister Tony Blair, as well as entertainers such as Elton John and Bono. The ICIJ would not identify the source of the leaked documents, which brought to light strategies for shielding assets worth trillions of dollars from tax authorities, regulators and creditors, truly emphasizing the widespread, systematic nature of financial secrecy and corruption across the globe.

Together, the trilogy highlighted the urgent need for financial transparency, and each of these investigations relied heavily on the power of AI to sift through massive amounts of data to uncover trends, anomalies and stories of global significance that may have taken humans years to detect, or possibly would have missed entirely.

While AI has yet to transform journalism in all the ways expected, it has revolutionized data journalism, as these tools can handle vast datasets that would be impossible for human reporters to analyze alone. [4] To that end, the collaboration between AI and journalists has led to more efficient and accurate reporting. This synergy was particularly evident during the Pandora Papers investigation, where advanced algorithms were used to analyze the nearly 12 million documents, allowing AI to process and cross-reference enormous volumes of data quickly and effectively. Machine learning algorithms were also used to identify connections between different entities and individuals, revealing a complex web of financial secrecy that would easily have been missed by human eyes.

1 International Consortium of Investigative Journalists (2016), 'The Panama Papers: Exposing the Rogue Offshore Finance Industry'. Retrieved from: icij.org/investigations/panama-papers/

2 International Consortium of Investigative Journalists (2017), 'The Paradise Papers: Secrets of the Global Elite'. Retrieved from: icij.org/investigations/paradise-papers/

Ethical concerns such as algorithm biases, data privacy and the accountability of AI systems are challenges journalists and publishers must carefully navigate, however. The sheer volume of data can also sometimes make it difficult for journalists to prioritize and verify findings. Yet the pros outweigh the cons, as the benefits of using AI in journalism, and in particular data journalism, are immense. The Panama, Paradise and Pandora Papers have had significant global impacts, leading to policy changes, resignations, criminal investigations and greater public awareness of the need for financial transparency. 5

As these technologies continue to evolve, AI's application in journalism is likely to expand, with future possibilities including more sophisticated data analysis tools, enhanced national language processing capabilities and improved methods of verifying information. This, in turn, can help reporters uncover more complex stories faster and with greater accuracy, ensuring journalism remains an integral piece in the puzzle of holding the powerful to account and keeping the public well informed.

3   International Consortium of Investigative Journalists (2021), 'Pandora Papers'. Retrieved from: icij.org/investigations/pandora-papers/

4   Shafer, J. (2024, February 27) 'How AI Is Already Transforming the News Business', Politico. Retrieved from: politico.com/news/magazine/2024/02/27/artificial-intelligence-media-00143508

5   Fitzgibbon, W. and Hudson, M. (2021, April 3) 'Five years later, Panama Papers still having a big impact', International Consortium of Investigative Journalists. Retrieved from: icij.org/investigations/panama-papers/five-years-later-panama-papers-still-having-a-big-impact/

Related terms

→   Data journalism
→   Machine learning
→   Natural Language Processing (NLP)
→   Big data
→   Financial crimes

Further reading

Bullough, O. (2018) Moneyland: Why Thieves and Crooks Now Rule the World and How to Take It Back. London: Profile Books.

Burgis, T. (2021) Kleptopia: How Dirty Money is Conquering the World. Glasgow: William Collins.

Obermaier, F. & Obermayer, B. (2017) The Panama Papers: Breaking the Story of How the Rich and Powerful Hide Their Money. London: Oneworld Publications.

Whistleblower

By Hannah Al Mannai

To blow the whistle on something or someone is an idiom that means to speak publicly about the internal secrets of a company, politician, government or an individual not following the law, ethics, governance or the promise they had pledged. There is no realm where this isn't prevalent, from oil and gas to state secrets. On some level, it is considered one of the main pillars of journalism; the goal to expose the truth of what goes on behind closed doors.

The concept of whistleblowing on behalf of your own government dates back to seventh-century England and qui tam, shortened from a Latin phrase that translates to "he who prosecutes for himself as well as for the King." [1] Modern lawmakers have adopted this term as synonymous with whistleblowers who sue corrupt companies on behalf of their authorities. The earliest example of this ruling stems from 695 AD, when King Wihtred of Kent declared: "If a freeman works during [the Sabbath], he shall forfeit his [profits], and the man who informs against him shall have half the fine, and [the profits] of the labor."

One of the first instances of whistleblowing in the USA came from Benjamin Franklin, considered to be the nation's founding father, in 1773, when he exposed confidential letters that stated the governor of Massachusetts had purposely misled parliament to promote a military build-up in the colonies. [2]

In 1917, the Espionage Act was established in the USA to criminalize any recording, pictures or copying of information related to the national defense being released with an intent to injure. This has since come under much scrutiny for its vague terms and has been used against whistleblowers who disclose government secrets to the press. [3] The Biden administration, for example, had been trying for years to extradite Wikileaks founder Julian Assange, so he can be tried under this law for leaking military secrets.

While the concept spans centuries, the term whistleblowing in its modern form took much longer to come into existence. One of its best-known first uses was by American political activist Ralph Nader, in 1971, who described it as: "An act of a man or woman who, believing that the public interest overrides the interest of the organization he serves, blows the whistle that the organization is involved in corrupt, illegal, fraudulent or harmful activity." [4]

Stories of individuals going up against organizations and states have been told across eras and nations. This includes Vladimir Bogdanovich Rezun, also known by his pseudonym Viktor Suvorov. [5] Suvorov was a former Soviet intelligence officer, who defected to the UK in 1978. In 1981, he exposed Soviet secrets in his memoirs. From the Arab world, Egyptian whistleblower Mohamed Ali exposed numerous videos of President Sisi and his circle's excessively luxurious lifestyles as citizens of Egypt suffered amid a devastating economic crisis. [6] There are hundreds, if not thousands, more examples of whistleblowing through the ages.

Whistleblowing and journalism go hand in hand, with a common goal of fighting corruption. The role of the journalist is to collaborate with those willing to expose the unlawful activities of an organization or group. Trust between the two parties is key, as whistleblowers take on a major risk, but a recent study at the University of Georgia showed many former whistleblowers have lost their faith in media, believing journalists no longer want change, nor that they keep their sources anonymous as they used to do. [7] On the other hand, journalists face the possibility of ruining their entire career for trusting the wrong source.

The advent of AI, however, could prove useful to both whistleblowers and journalists. Automated data analysis, for example, can make it easier to gather evidence of corruption, while predictive analytics can also predict potential risks and flag suspicious activities before they turn more sinister. Journalistic tools such as

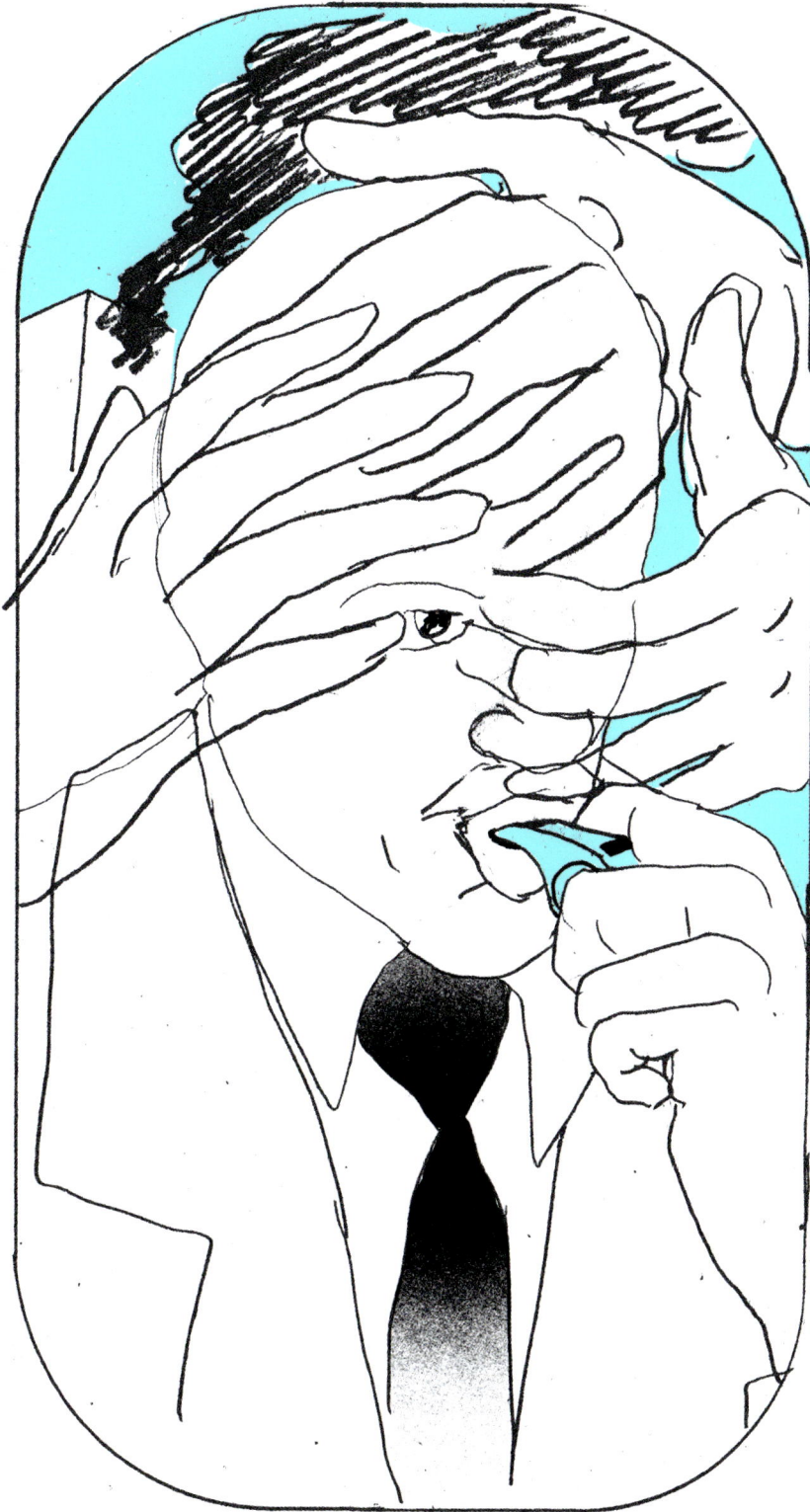

1 Whistleblowing History Overview. Retrieved from: whistleblowersinternational.com/what-is-whistleblowing/whistleblowing-history-overview/

2 Ibid.

3 Risen, J. (2022, July 12) 'Rashida Tlaib Is Trying to Fix the Espionage Act, but Whistleblowers Are Probably Out of Luck', The Intercept. Retrieved from: theintercept.com/2022/07/12/whistleblower-espionage-act-reform/

those for fact-checking can help reporters verify a source's information. AI can also facilitate collaboration between journalists and the public, including whistleblowers, by crowdsourcing information and using machine learning to analyze contributions, identifying credible leads and stories.

At the same time, AI-driven platforms can provide secure and anonymous channels using encryption or blockchain technology for whistleblowers to report misconduct without fear of retaliation. This includes SecureDrop, an open-source whistleblower submission system used by media organizations to securely accept documents from anonymous sources.

Of course, we must also consider the ethical and legal implications of AI usage in these investigative reports, particularly concerning privacy, data security and the potential for misuse of these technologies. The onus is now on journalists and organizations who must navigate these challenges carefully to maintain trust and credibility.

Ultimately, the intersection of AI, whistleblowing and journalism represents a powerful convergence of technology and ethics that can continue to promote transparency, accountability and an informed public discourse.

Related terms

→ Whistleblower protection
→ Confidential informant
→ Corporate transparency
→ Ethical breach
→ Investigative journalism
→ Non-Disclosure Agreement (NDA)
→ Public interest disclosure

Further reading

Mueller, T. (2021) Crisis of Conscience: Whistleblowing in an Age of Fraud. London: Atlantic Books.

Snowden, E. (2020) Permanent Record: A Memoir of a Reluctant Whistleblower. London: Pan Macmillan.

Gosztola, K. (2023) Guilty of Journalism: The Political Prosecution of Julian Assange. New York: Seven Stories Press, U.S.

4 Banisar, D. (2011, February) 'Whistleblowing: International Standards and Developments' in Corruption And Transparency: Debating The Frontiers Between State, Market And Society, I. Sandoval, ed. Washington, D.C.: World Bank-Institute for Social Research.

5 Garthoff, R. L. (1984) [Review of Memoirs.; Inside the Soviet Army, by P. G. Grigorenko & V. Suvorov], Political Science Quarterly, 99(1), 93–94. Retrieved from: doi.org/10.2307/2150260

6 Saba, J (2019, September 24) 'Mohamed Ali: The self-exiled Egyptian sparking protests at home', BBC. Retrieved from: bbc.com/news/world-middle-east-49800212 Fix the Espionage Act, but Whistleblowers Are Probably Out of Luck', The Intercept. Retrieved from: theintercept.com/2022/07/12/whistleblower-espionage-act-reform/

7 Techo, E. (2023, March 7) 'Whistleblowers losing faith in media impact', University of Georgia. Retrieved from: news.uga.edu/whistleblowers-mistrust-journalism/

2

Surveillance

Verification

Oversight

Bias

By Salim Al-Shuaili

A facial recognition algorithm that over-represents white people or security data that infuses racial bias in AI policing tools—these are just two of the ways bias in AI could have profound implications on human lives.

This issue is becoming critical, having garnered significant attention as AI systems become increasingly integrated into various aspects of our daily lives, including media and journalism. It refers to the presence of prejudices or favoritism in AI algorithms and models, which can lead to unfair, discriminatory or inaccurate outcomes. This bias can stem from multiple sources, including the data used to train AI models, the design of algorithms and the human oversight involved in developing these systems.

How does it happen?

One of the most significant sources of bias is via data that is used to train AI models. Often, it is not representative of the broader population or contains inherent prejudices. For instance, if an AI system is trained on historical data that reflects societal biases, such as gender or racial discrimination, it is likely to perpetuate those biases. An example is the underrepresentation of minority groups in training datasets, which can result in AI systems that perform poorly for these groups.

Algorithmic bias, meanwhile, arises from the way AI algorithms are designed and implemented. Even with unbiased data, the design choices made by developers can introduce partiality. For instance, an algorithm might prioritize certain features over others, leading to skewed results. Additionally, the lack of diversity among AI developers can contribute to biased perspectives being embedded into the algorithms.

The deployment of AI systems can also introduce bias, such as when one is used in media and journalism to filter news articles, it might prioritize certain types of content based on user preferences, leading to the reinforcement of existing biases. This is also known as an echo chamber. Similarly, the feedback loop created by user interactions with AI systems can perpetuate biased outcomes. On social media, for example, content that generates high engagement is promoted more, leading to even higher engagement.

What does it mean?

The presence of bias in AI could have a significant impact on humanity, particularly in fields like media and journalism, where the dissemination of information plays a crucial role in shaping public opinion. For example, biased AI systems can contribute to the spread of misinformation and disinformation by amplifying certain viewpoints while suppressing others. This can lead to a distorted perception of reality among the public and erode trust in media institutions.

AI systems that exhibit bias can also reinforce and even exacerbate existing societal inequalities. Biased algorithms in hiring processes can lead to discrimination against certain demographic groups, for example, while biased AI in law enforcement can result in unfair targeting of minority communities. Meanwhile, media organizations that rely on biased AI systems risk losing their credibility and trustworthiness if audiences believe that the information being presented is biased or unfair, leading to a decline in viewership and readership.

What do we do?

Addressing bias in AI requires a multifaceted approach that involves various stakeholders, including AI developers, policymakers and end-users. One key strategy would be to use training datasets that are diverse and representative of the broader population. This involves collecting data from a wide range of sources and regularly updating datasets to reflect changing demographics and societal norms.

Developing AI systems that are transparent and explainable can help identify and address biases. Transparency involves making the data, algorithms and decision-making processes of AI systems accessible to scrutiny, while explainability refers to the ability to understand and interpret the process that produced the outcomes of AI models.

Incorporating ethical considerations into the AI development process can also help prevent the introduction of biases, including involving diverse teams in the development process, conducting bias audits, and implementing ethical guidelines and standards. Policymakers can play a significant role in mitigating bias by implementing regulations and oversight mechanisms, such as setting standards for data collection and usage, requiring regular audits of AI systems and enforcing accountability measures for biased outcomes.

Once these AI systems are in place, the work does not end, as these should be continuously monitored for biased outcomes, and feedback mechanisms should be in place to address any issues that arise. This involves collecting feedback from users and stakeholders and making necessary adjustments to the AI models and algorithms.

Ultimately, bias in AI is a complex and multifaceted issue that requires concerted efforts to address. As AI systems continue to play an increasingly prominent role in media and journalism, it is imperative to understand and mitigate the inherent biases that can arise. By adopting diverse data practices, ensuring transparency, incorporating ethical considerations, implementing regulatory measures and continuously monitoring AI systems, we can work towards creating AI that is fair, unbiased and trustworthy. The goal is to harness the power of AI to enhance, rather than undermine, the equitable dissemination of information and the creation of a more informed and just society.

Related terms

→ Algorithmic bias
→ Data bias
→ Echo chamber
→ Transparency in AI
→ Explainability in AI
→ Ethical AI development
→ Bias audits
→ Regulatory oversight
→ Feedback loops
→ Societal inequalities
→ Diverse training data

Further reading

Broussard, M. (2023) More Than a Glitch: Confronting Race, Gender, and Ability Bias in Tech. Cambridge (MA): MIT Press.

Criado Perez, C. (2019) Invisible Women: Exposing Data Bias in a World Designed for Men. New York: Abrams Press.

Eubanks, V. (2018) Automating Inequality: How High-Tech Tools Profile, Police, and Punish the Poor. New York: St. Martin's Press.

Noble, S. U. (2018) Algorithms of Oppression: How Search Engines Reinforce Racism. New York: NYU Press.

Drones

By Rashid Al-Mohanadi

It is the year 2050. The AI revolution is akin to the industrial revolution in the 20th century, but what once made it revolutionary has now become ordinary. In the best part of the 20th century, 'digital' was a term used to describe almost any new technology based on computing. Now, AI has replaced that.

Drones powered by AI on land, air and sea now conduct most aspects of the global transport and logistics industries. Our airliners whisk people from continent to continent autonomously. Our oil and LNG are shipped using unmanned tankers and unloaded into ports using unmanned receiving terminals. Our cities are dominated by flying autonomous vehicles, making traffic jams and human-error accidents a thing of the past. Our wars are fought using AI-powered drones, minimizing human casualties in most conflicts but drastically lowering the old barriers of war. However, this is a story for another piece.

Historically, the use of AI and drones has been in labor-intensive and repetitive jobs like construction, manufacturing and managing infrastructure. But a recent change is more eerie, more diabolical, and, in its essence, challenges the structural building blocks of human societies...

In the bustling metropolis of Metropol-AI, skyscrapers kiss the clouds, and the hum of technology is omnipresent. Humans and drones roam the landscape, working hand in hand for the betterment of society. One of the areas the AI revolution has transformed is journalism. Gone are the days when human journalists ran around the streets, journal and pen in hand, acting as the gatekeepers of truth. Now, AI-powered drones have replaced almost all human reporters, ensuring the unfiltered, raw truth is broadcast to the masses rather than the biases and whims of a few journalists.

Emancipating, isn't it?

Do not be tricked by the façade; the truth is not as bright. The fact is most of the drones are owned by one man: Victor Nicol-AI, one of the moguls who invested in AI-powered drone journalism technology in the 2020s. He now runs the largest media networks and platforms. Using his drones, he can alter the truth in the interest of the highest bidder. The fact that truth can be bought is not new, but we have never witnessed the procurement of truth on such a scale. With Victor's journalistic drone fleet, a protest for justice can be portrayed as a riot of chaos; a peaceful demonstration can be depicted as a threat to national security. The truth has become malleable and tailored to the likings of Victor and his patrons.

Human advancement has been based on seeking the truth, but now the truth has eroded, and the lines between fact and fiction have blurred.

Yet, among the turmoil and chaos, a flicker of hope looms. A renegade band of human journalists, disillusioned by the disinformation of Victor Nicol-AI and his army of drones, have sought to bring back ethical journalism. They are determined to claw back the tide of distorted truth using the technology that disposed of them in the first place. Hacking Victor's AI-powered drones, the renegade bunch will ultimately project the unaltered truth and expose Victor Nicol-AI's tricks to the masses, revealing the manipulations that lay beneath the surface.

The journalists' mission is a dangerous one. With limited resources and nowhere to hide, they wage a silent war against the manipulators of truth. They fight this battle not only for the future of journalism but for the pure essence of truth and human advancement, ensuring that the power of the truth is in the hands of many and not in the clutches of a few.

Technology will only
emancipate us
if it is liberated.

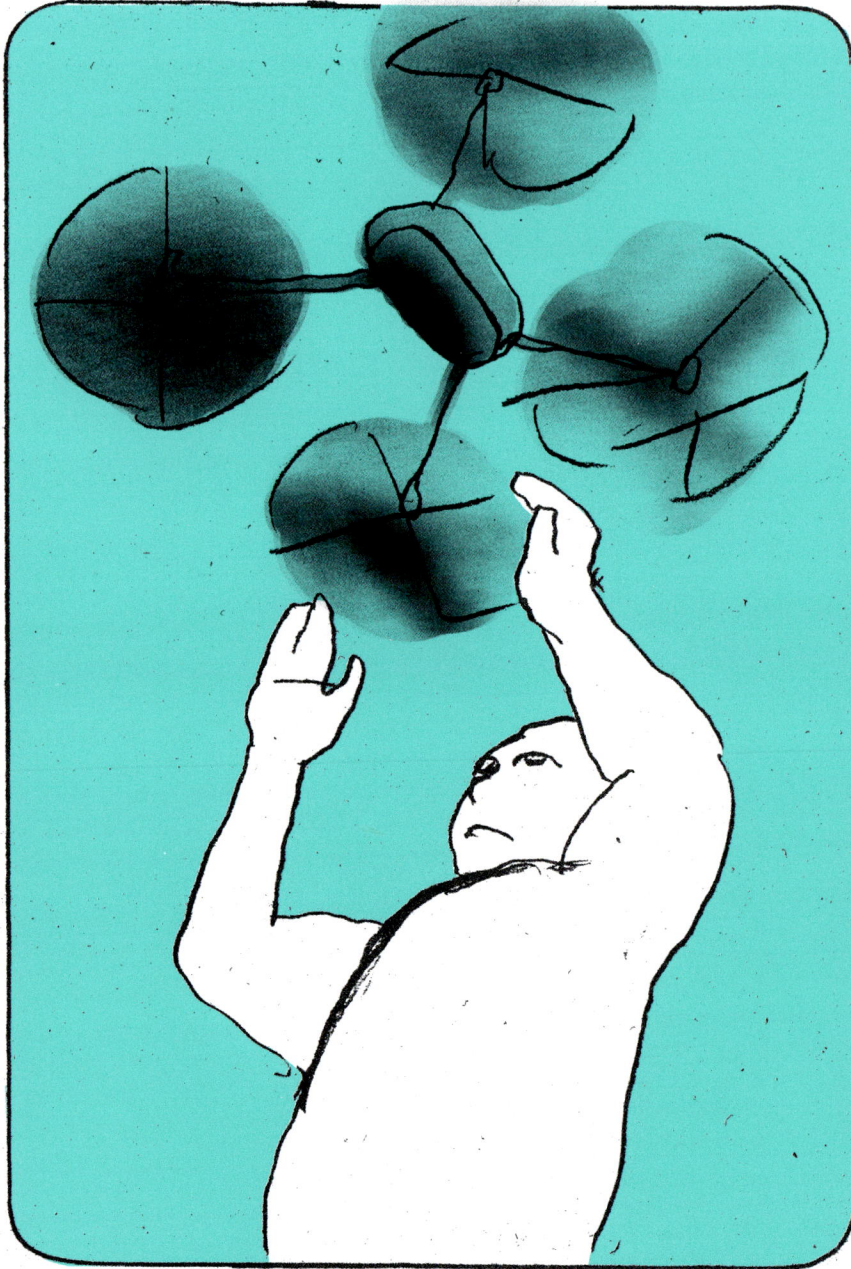

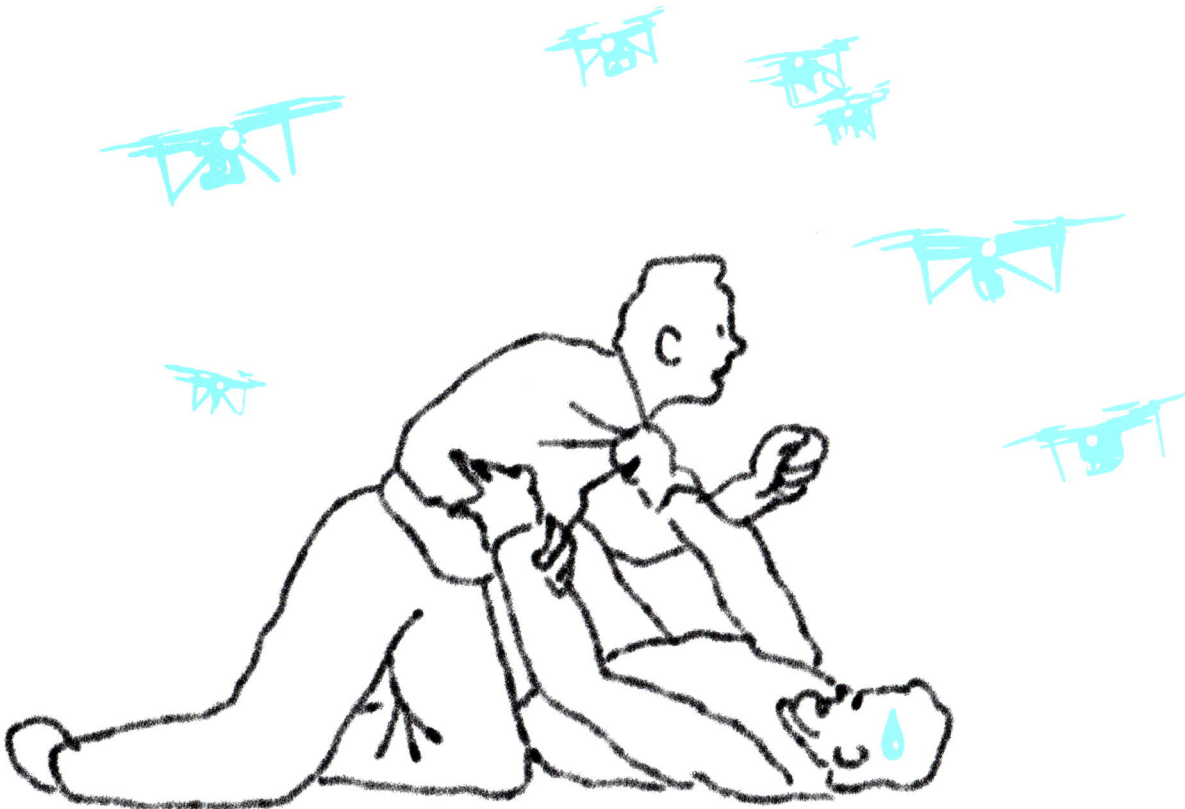

Related terms

→ Unmanned Aerial Vehicle (UAV)
→ Aerial photography
→ Drone journalism
→ Remote sensing
→ Real-time reporting
→ Crowdsourcing

Further reading

Brose, C. (2020) The Kill Chain: Defending America in the Future of High-Tech Warfare. New York: Hachette Books.

Scharre, P. (2018) Army of None: Autonomous Weapons and the Future of War. New York: W. W. Norton & Company.

Singer, P. W. (2009) Wired for War: The Robotics Revolution and Conflict in the 21st Century. New York: Penguin Books.

Hallucination

By Sashreek Garg

How humans can see figures in the clouds or faces on the Moon, similarly AI systems can perceive patterns or objects that are non-existent, creating outputs that are nonsensical or completely inaccurate. These are called AI hallucinations, and they can have far more significant consequences for real-world applications than a human spotting the 'man in the Moon.'

AI hallucinations occur when a system generates false information or factual errors despite being trained on extensive datasets. These errors have far-reaching effects, impacting AI ethics, reliability and user trust in AI-powered platforms. These occurrences highlight the need for rigorous fact-checking and human oversight in developing and deploying AI technologies.

A few examples of AI hallucinations are when Google's Bard chatbot incorrectly claimed the James Webb Space Telescope had captured the world's first images of a planet outside our solar system.[1] Or when Microsoft's chat AI, Sydney, stated that is was falling in love with users and spying on Bing employees.[2] Meta pulled its Galactica LLM demo altogether after just three days back in 2022 after it provided users with inaccurate information, some rooted in prejudice.[3]

How do they come about?

AI hallucinations can be influenced by various factors during the model's training and operational framework, leading to incorrect or misleading outputs. AI models depend heavily on the data they are trained on. If this training data is biased or unrepresentative, the AI may develop skewed perceptions that lead to hallucinations. For instance, a facial recognition system trained predominantly on images of faces from one ethnicity may misidentify individuals from other ethnicities.

While they are capable of handling complex tasks, AI models, which are trained to predict, can sometimes make incorrect assumptions or interpretations. This complexity leads to the generation of outputs that defy human intuition or logic. The complicated structure of these models can misrepresent or fabricate data to reconcile with their flawed assumptions or ill-suited structures.[4]

There's also something called overfitting, which occurs when an AI model is trained too closely on its training data, memorizing details and noise instead of learning to generalize. This can cause the model to perform poorly on new, unseen data, often hallucinating irrelevant patterns or trends. An example of this would be a stock prediction model that is unable to adapt to new market conditions because it was overly fitted to historical data. Additionally, AI models are susceptible to adversarial attacks, where malicious inputs designed to confuse the AI can lead to incorrect outputs.

What are the consequences?

The dissemination of false information and creation of security vulnerabilities are two crucial consequences of AI hallucinations. These issues not only impact individual decisions but also have broader societal implications. For example, instances of AI-generated misinformation can influence public opinion and decision-making processes. AI hallucinations in news bots might spread unchecked falsehoods during emergencies, potentially aggravating situations rather than aiding in their resolution. Similarly, a healthcare AI model might misdiagnose a condition based on biased data, leading to unnecessary medical procedures and causing physical, emotional and financial strain on patients.

AI hallucinations also pose substantial security risks, particularly in the fields of technology and cybersecurity. Malicious actors can exploit these vulnerabilities to launch attacks, such as documented cases where AI recommended non-existent software packages, leading to potential breaches in data security.

How can we prevent them?

To mitigate AI hallucinations, it is important to use high-quality, diverse and comprehensive training data. This involves curating datasets that accurately represent real-world scenarios and are free as possible from biases and errors. Regular updates and expansions of the dataset can help the AI adapt to new information and reduce inaccuracies.

Clearly defining the purpose and limitations of AI models is also important, so AI systems can focus on generating relevant and reliable outputs, minimizing irrelevant or misleading results. Incorporating human oversight also remains a critical step in the validation process of AI outputs. Human reviewers can identify and correct inaccuracies that AI may overlook, improving the accuracy of AI-generated content and ensuring its relevance and reliability before being utilized or published.

AI hallucinations will likely remain an ongoing challenge as models become more sophisticated. Future AI systems may develop supplemental fact-checking capabilities, potentially providing real-time access to verified databases. We might see AI models that can express degrees of certainty about their outputs, flagging responses that are less reliable. Some researchers are exploring multi-model approaches, where different AI systems cross-check each other's work, creating a network of AI fact-checkers. Additionally, advancements in explainable AI can help users understand the reasoning behind AI-generated information, making it easier to identify potential hallucinations.

As our understanding of AI cognition deepens, we may be able to develop more nuanced strategies for mitigating hallucinations, perhaps even leveraging the creative potential of AI 'imagination' in some fields while distinguishing it from fact.

[1] Metz, C. (2023, March 29) 'What Makes A.I. Chatbots Go Wrong?', The New York Times. Retrieved from: nytimes.com/2023/03/29/technology/ai-chatbots-hallucinations.html

[2] Neto, J. A. R. (2023, March 15) 'ChatGPT and the Generative AI Hallucinations', Medium. Retrieved from: medium.com/chatgpt-learning/chatgtp-and-the-generative-ai-hallucinations-62feddc72369

[3] Heaven, W. D. (2022, November 18) 'Why Meta's latest large language model survived only three days online', MIT Technology Review. Retrieved from: technologyreview.com/2022/11/18/1063487/meta-large-language-model-ai-only-survived-three-days-gpt-3-science/

[4] Benati, M. (2024, June 25) 'Understanding AI Hallucinations: Causes and Prevention', LinkedIn. Retrieved from: https://www.linkedin.com/pulse/understanding-ai-hallucinations-causes-prevention-marcello-benati-sob5c/

Related terms

→ Fabrication
→ Model error
→ Data artifact
→ Confabulation
→ False positive
→ Incoherent output
→ Overfitting
→ Spurious correlation

Further reading

Rodewald, J. (2023). AI Hallucinations Decoded: A Practical Guide for Everyday Users to Master and Avoid AI Missteps. Independently published.

Katherine Johnson

By Jasmina Bondare

It was an offhand conversation between Margot Lee Shetterly and her father that allowed Katherine Johnson's story into the public consciousness. [1] Today, we know Johnson (1918–2020) was one of the most influential women of color in STEM, her groundbreaking work in mathematics often linked to modern AI, but her many triumphs and challenges were almost entirely lost to history, if it weren't for this chance encounter.

As Shetterly's father, a climate research scientist who worked at NASA's Langley Research Center, spoke about his former colleague Johnson, Shetterly wondered, "Why haven't I heard about her before?" That spurred her to research and write her bestselling 2016 book Hidden Figures, which shares the untold story of the Black women mathematicians who helped America win the Space Race, later turned into an award-winning film starring Octavia Spencer, Janelle Monáe and Kevin Costner.

Johnson was a mathematician at NASA and, despite facing racial and gender barriers, her work was critical in early space missions such as Alan Shepard's 1961 mission 'Freedom 7' and John Glenn's 1962 mission 'Friendship 7'. Her calculations helped send the first Americans into space, and she was honored with the Presidential Medal of Freedom in 2015. [2]

So, why did it take so long for the world to learn her name?

The birth of a legend

Johnson was born in White Sulfur Springs, West Virginia, in 1918. She showed signs of being gifted from a young age. She was ready for high school by the age of 10 but was unable to attend in her area because there was a lack of facilities open to Black people at that time. Determined to give her a chance to succeed, her father rented a home in a neighboring county where she could further her education. She graduated at 14 and went to West Virginia State College, a historically Black university, excelling in every mathematics course she took. Even so, Johnson faced significant challenges after entering the science field.

During this period, both women and African Americans were actively fighting for their rights in the USA. Johnson witnessed drastic societal changes throughout her life, from Women's Suffrage in 1920, which granted women the right to vote, to the Civil Rights Movement in the 1950s and 1960s, which saw people fight for social justice and equality for African Americans. Despite these changes, by the time Johnson was entering the job field, it was difficult for a woman, especially a Black woman, to be given the opportunity to do more than behind-the-scenes work. So, she joined the group of 'human computers,' Black women whose jobs were to check the white men's calculations at NASA. It was not until NASA was scrambling to win the Space Race that Johnson got her opportunity to truly shine.

The race to space

The Space Race was a competition between the Soviet Union and the USA, when the two battled it out to achieve superior spaceflight capabilities. Both giants had locked horns, attempting to be the first to space. The Soviets ultimately beat the USA when cosmonaut Yuri Gagarin became the first person to ever orbit Earth in April 1961. The USA, meanwhile, was trying to find someone who could do the calculations necessary to send a man into space—yet kept failing. They asked every white man in the department, but none could crack the code. That's when they looked to their human computers and specifically Johnson.

Weeks after Gagarin reached space, Alan Shepard became the first American to go into the great unknown and the person behind the calculation that got him there was Johnson. She became so entrusted by her team it was said that John Glenn would no longer trust the computers' calculations. "If she says they're good, then I'm ready to go," he said of Johnson. [3]

As with Alan Turing and his team of Enigma codebreakers (see more on page 76), the contributions of Johnson underscore the importance of precise computation and problem-solving skills that are foundational to AI.

Yet Johnson's story, like those of many women and people of color, particularly from those decades, might have remained untold if not for that offhand conversation between Shetterly and her father. This only serves to highlight the imbalance in the narratives we hear. This discrepancy between the people who are known emphasizes the importance of journalism and storytelling in giving those who are voiceless a voice and ensuring that all contributions, no matter a person's background, are acknowledged.

By honoring hidden figures in history such as Katherine Johnson, we encourage more women and people of color to inspire change, knowing their achievements will not be forgotten.

1   Rechtoris, M. (2020, January 16) 'Hidden Figures' Margot Lee Shetterly: How Writing Is a lot Like e-Discovery', Relativity. Retrieved from: relativity.com/blog/hidden-figures-margot-lee-shetterly-how-writing-is-a-lot-like-e-discovery/

2   Deiss, H. (2020, February 24) 'Katherine Johnson: A Lifetime of STEM', NASA. Retrieved from: nasa.gov/learning-resources/katherine-johnson-a-lifetime-of-stem/

3   Shetterly, M. L. (2016, November 22) 'Katherine Johnson Biography', NASA. Retrieved from: nasa.gov/centers-and-facilities/langley/katherine-johnson-biography/

Related terms

→   Science, technology, engineering and mathematics (STEM)
→   Segregation
→   Civil rights
→   Empowerment
→   Social justice
→   Equality
→   Human computers
→   Space Race

Further reading

Holt, N. (2016) Rise of the Rocket Girls: The Women Who Propelled Us, from Missiles to the Moon to Mars. Boston: Little, Brown and Company.

Johnson, K., et al. (2021) My Remarkable Journey: A Memoir. New York: Amistad.

Paul, R., & Moss, S. (2015) We Could not Fail: The First African Americans in the Space Program. Austin: University Of Texas Press.

Bradford Edwards, S. & Harris, D. (2017) Hidden Human Computers: The Black Women of NASA. Minneapolis: ABDO.

Lovelace, Lovelock

By Katy Gillett

While AI has become the next frontier in technology, it is the visionary human minds behind its creation that have left an indelible mark on the field. Two such figures, Ada Lovelace and James Lovelock, are among those who shaped its foundations, guiding its evolution. Their work, driven by a love for science and discovery, undeniably helped pave the way for modern AI.

Lovelace's influence on AI

Ada Lovelace, the daughter of famous poet Lord Byron, is regarded in history books as the world's first computer programmer, as she wrote the first algorithm intended for a machine. After being inspired by her friend, the mathematician Charles Babbage, who designed a calculating machine called the Difference Engine, in 1843, she translated a French paper about the Analytical Engine and, in her own annotations, published how it could perform a sequence of calculations. [1] This became the first computer program, although the Analytical Engine was never finished and Lovelace never did receive the adequate recognition she deserved for her achievements.

Her most famous work, Translator's Note A, emphasized that the Analytical Engine could act upon anything that could be expressed in symbols, an idea central to the development of AI, where data and operations extend beyond arithmetic to include complex algorithms capable of learning and adapting.

She had laid the groundwork for modern computing, as she envisioned machines capable of more than mere calculations. She predicted their potential to create music, art and more. But she also maintained a critical stance on AI's limitations, famously arguing that machines could only execute what they were programmed to do, only what humans know how to do and could not originate anything on their own. [2] This perspective was dubbed by Alan Turing (see page 76 for more) as Lady Lovelace's Objection and continues to influence discussions about the nature and limits of AI even today. So much so, that in 2001 the Lovelace Test was proposed to assess whether a machine can demonstrate creativity independently of human input, a challenge AI has arguably yet to meet.

Lovelock's Gaia and Novacene theories

Chemist and inventor James Lovelock, meanwhile, was best known for the Gaia hypothesis, alongside biologist Lynn Margulis. [3] It was named after the ancient Greek goddess of Earth and introduced in the early 1970s. Briefly, their theory was that Earth and its biological systems behave as a singular entity, closely controlling self-regulatory negative feedback loops that keep conditions on the planet within boundaries that are favorable to life.

This hypothesis of co-evolution of biology and the physical environment, where each influences the other, claims the power of biology to control the non-living environment. The approach influenced how we understand complex systems, including AI, as Lovelock's vision of Earth as a self-regulating system parallels the principles of AI systems that learn and adapt.

Lovelock's more recent Novacene theory posits that we are transitioning from the Anthropocene epoch to a new era called the Novacene, where AI will emerge as a dominant force, vastly surpassing human intelligence. [4] Quite unlike Lovelace's belief about the limitations of AI beyond those of humans, Lovelock envisions these new AI entities, or cyborgs, as capable of thinking 10,000 times faster than humans. But he believes these hyper-intelligent beings will not seek to destroy humanity, but instead work to preserve the planet, recognizing the interdependence of all life forms.

Lovelock suggests these AI entities will act as benevolent caretakers of Earth, helping to mitigate the effects of climate change and other environmental threats. He argues that the development of AI is a natural progression in the evolution of intelligence and that these entities will be essential for the long-term survival of life on Earth.

Lovelace meets Lovelock

Lovelace's foresight into the capabilities of algorithms and Lovelock's understanding of adaptive systems are essential premises that underpin the creation of AI systems today. Applications of AI in journalism and across various industries reflect Lovelace's vision of machines capable of creative and meaningful tasks, and Lovelock's principles of adaptation. AI has yet to achieve autonomy, as Lovelace predicted, but its future potential, which Lovelock believes is vast, is yet to be fully realized.

There is no doubt that Lovelace's legacy will continue to inspire innovations in algorithm design for a long time to come, pushing the boundaries of what AI can achieve in content creation and analysis. Lovelock's interdisciplinary approach, meanwhile, will also guide the development of AI systems that are not only intelligent but also ethical and sustainable, and, hopefully, particularly useful in saving this planet of humans that created the technology in the first place.

1 Lovelace, A. A. (1843) 'Notes by AAL [August Ada Lovelace]', Scientific Memoirs, Taylor, R., ed. London, 3, 666–731.

2 Zwolak, J. (2023, March 22) 'Ada Lovelace: The World's First Computer Programmer Who Predicted Artificial Intelligence', National Institute of Standards and Technology. Retrieved from: nist.gov/blogs/taking-measure/ada-lovelace-worlds-first-computer-programmer-who-predicted-artificial

3 Lovelock, J. (2000) Gaia: A New Look at Life on Earth. Oxford: Oxford University Press.

4 Lovelock, J. (2019) Novacene: The Coming Age of Hyperintelligence. London: Penguin Books.

Related terms

- → Algorithms
- → Cybernetics
- → Adaptive systems
- → Modern computing

Further reading

Essinger, J. (2014) Ada's Algorithm: How Lord Byron's Daughter Ada Lovelace Launched the Digital Age. New York: Melville House.

Isaacson, W. (2015) The Innovators: How a Group of Hackers, Geniuses, and Geeks Created the Digital Revolution. New York: Simon & Schuster.

Lovelock, J. (2000) Gaia: A New Look at Life on Earth. Oxford: Oxford University Press.

Surveillance

By Farjana Salahuddin

The earliest form of surveillance was perhaps wiretapping during the Civil War in nineteenth-century USA, when both the Union and Confederacy tapped into each other's telegraph lines and copied down the messages. [1] It has come a long way since then, with the introduction of CCTVs, GPS, smartphones and biometrics.

Surveillance is defined as an act of monitoring and observing actions of a person, an organization or others, in order to gather data and information. [2] In today's world, with the prevalence of mobile devices, internet and our love of connectivity, new means of surveillance are emerging all the time, resulting in both positive and negative implications.

The act of surveillance can be divided into two categories: covert and overt. Covert surveillance refers to the techniques used where the subjects are unaware they are being watched or heard, while overt surveillance is when they are aware and can recognize the devices watching them—for example, CCTV cameras. [3]

How are we being surveilled?

Here are six types of surveillance widely used during investigations: [4]

→ Physical: The subject, their actions and locations are observed in person.

→ Electronic: Technology, like cameras, microphones, etc., are utilized to gather information.

→ Computer: Monitoring of online activities, internet browsing history, emails and so on, to observe a subject's actions.

→ Social media: Monitoring the subjects' activity on social media to gather information about their activities, interests and contacts.

→ Financial: Tracking financial transactions of the subject to find patterns, suspicious transactions, criminal activity and illicit behavior.

→ Biometric: Tracking subjects based on their physical characteristics, such as fingerprints, or identifying a person on CCTV and their movement using face recognition.

1 Wu, T. et al., (n.d.) 'The Ethics (or not) of Massive Government Surveillance', Stanford University Computer Science. Retrieved from: cs.stanford.edu/people/eroberts/cs181/projects/ethics-of-surveillance/history_19century.html

2 Lyon, D. (2001) Surveillance Society: Monitoring in Everyday Life. Philadelphia: Open University Press.

3 'What are the Different Types of Surveillance?' (2020), Esoteric. Retrieved from: esotericltd.com/2020/09/11/what-are-the-different-types-of-surveillance/

4 '6 Types of Surveillance for Investigations Explained' (2023, April 25), Investigate Academy. Retrieved from: investigativeacademy.com/6-types-of-surveillance-for-investigations-explained/

5 Biscop, M., Décary-Hétu, D. (2022) 'Anonymity technologies in investigative journalism: a tool for inspiring trust in sources', CrimRxiv. Retrieved from: crimrxiv.com/pub/5q86cefc/release/1

6 O'Carroll, L. (2023) 'Draft EU plans to allow spying on journalists are dangerous, warn critics', The Guardian. Retrieved from: theguardian.com/world/2023/jun/22/draft-eu-plans-to-allow-spying-on-journalists-are-dangerous-warn-critics

7 'Media Freedom Act: a new bill to protect EU journalists and press freedom' (2024, March 13), European Parliament. Retrieved from: europarl.europa.eu/news/en/press-room/20240308IPR19014/media-freedom-act-a-new-bill-to-protect-eu-journalists-and-press-freedom

8 Robinson, K. (2022) 'How Israel's Pegasus Spyware Stoked the Surveillance Debate', Council on Foreign Relations. Retrieved from: https://www.cfr.org/in-brief/how-israels-pegasus-spyware-stoked-surveillance-debate

The implications on journalism

In the realm of investigative journalism, surveillance and new digital and covert technologies are threatening reporters' reach, as well as the privacy, protection and mental well-being of journalists and their sources. [5] Journalists are increasingly becoming the target of surveillance, as their investigations can reveal discomforting truths about powerful individuals, corporations or governments. In 2023, EU leaders prepared a draft legislation that authorized the use of spying on journalists by national security agencies, a move vilified by the media at the time. [6] Later on, in 2024, the European Parliament adopted a final revised version of the Media Freedom Act that bans the use of spyware against journalists, except in strictly defined cases. In such cases, the journalist would be made aware any surveillance has taken place. [7]

That said, covert instances of spying have been widely acknowledged. For example, in 2021, there was an unprecedented leak of 50,000 phone numbers that had been selected for surveillance on Pegasus, a military-grade surveillance software created by NSO Group, a company headquartered in Israel. [8] Further investigations have shown it was also used to hack the phones of a dozen US diplomats who were using foreign numbers while working abroad.

The foremost ethical concern of the emergence of such surveillance tools is the threat to press freedom, and the loss of trust between journalists and sources. Anybody may be under surveillance without their knowledge, thus exposing the sources and leading to potential threats and being silenced by any means. [9]

Savvier and savvier

The rise of new technologies and means of mass surveillance during COVID-19 to curtail the pandemic were also later repurposed or misused by authorities. For example, an AP investigation called Tracked found authorities using COVID-era data and technology to curtail travel for activists and ordinary people, harass marginalized groups and connect health information to other surveillance and law enforcement tools in ways no one had anticipated. In some cases, data was also shared with spy agencies. [10]

The developments in new technologies have created even more discrete means of surveillance, such as spyware that can infiltrate a subject's phone with zero-click attacks, whereby the user doesn't need to click on any links for the device to get infiltrated. [11]

While there are many good uses for surveillance—such as the use of CCTV for crime reduction, providing real-time information to first responders in emergency situations, for workplace safety, traffic monitoring, wildlife conservation and so on—it has quickly become a tactic to impose regulations on the way information is curated for the public to consume. [12] This definition, or re-definition, brings a chilling narrative to journalism, as well as the entire world, on how our world's perception may be impacted—or worse, constructed.

9   Biscop, M., Décary-Hétu, D. (2022) 'Anonymity technologies in investigative journalism: a tool for inspiring trust in sources', CrimRxiv. Retrieved from: crimrxiv.com/pub/5q86cefc/release/1

10   Burke, G. et al (2022, December 20) 'Police seize on COVID-19 tech to expand global surveillance', AP Special Projects. Retrieved from: apspecialprojects. com/police-seize-on-covid-19-tech-to-expand-global-surveillance

11   'What is zero-click malware, and how do zero-click attacks work?' (n.d.) Kaspersky. Retrieved from: me-en.kaspersky.com/resource-center/definitions/what-is-zero-click-malware

12   Mills, A. (2018) 'Now You See Me – Now You Don't: Journalists' Experiences With Surveillance', Journalism Practice, Volume 13, Issue 6. Retrieved from: tandfonline. com/doi/pdf/10.1080/17512786.2018.1555006

Related terms

→   Espionage
→   Wire tap
→   Bug
→   Blackhat
→   Zero-click
→   Pegasus
→   Infiltration

Further reading

Lyon, D. (2001) Surveillance Society: Monitoring Everyday Life. Buckingham: Open University Press.

Park, Y. J. (2021) The Future of Digital Surveillance: Why Digital Monitoring Will Never Lose Its Appeal in a World of Algorithm-Driven AI. Ann Arbor: University of Michigan Press.

Zuboff, S. (2019) The Age of Surveillance Capitalism: The Fight for a Human Future at the New Frontier of Power. New York: PublicAffairs.

Verification

By Marc Owen Jones

Is it possible to be lied to by people who do not even exist? Without verification, it is. In 2020, over 46 different publications across the globe published about 90 articles by journalists who used AI-generated or stolen photos as their avatars. The fake journalists charmed and tricked the editors with fake social media profiles, bios and more.[1] Yet all it would have taken to avoid this, was if the editors had a video call with the journalists. They didn't. Even those who should know best did not follow a fundamental rule—before verifying the facts, verify the person exists.

A key component

Verification is a crucial journalistic process that assesses the credibility and reliability of information before publication. It involves gathering, evaluating and contextualizing evidence, while maintaining transparency about sources and limitations. It is the cornerstone of journalistic practice, enabling reporters, citizen journalists and netizens to ascertain the veracity and precision of news occurrences. This process grants journalists a distinctive claim to objectively interpret reality, thereby establishing their authority and status. As Kovach and Rosenstiel say, "In the end, the discipline of verification is what separates journalism from entertainment, propaganda, fiction, or art…".[2] Lofty discussions of journalism's role in upholding democracy or other political systems are subject to academic debate, verification, however, is fairly universal.

Verification has never been more vital to modern journalism, especially in the digital realm. The digital age has 'democratized' but also de-professionalized news gathering, with diverse actors now participating in the creation and dissemination of information. While the rise of citizen journalism has seen a proliferation of independent voices, there is a dark side. Populist politicians, social media and the decline of funding for journalism, have all contributed to a process of 'truth decay.'[3] This shift has led to a 'post-truth' environment where distinguishing fact from fiction has become even more challenging for citizens. Ideological conflicts and polarization, from Ukraine to Gaza, have also prompted blinkered reporting, where one's own views, journalists or otherwise, cloud interpretation of facts. Confirmation bias can cloud out objectivity, especially in an information age where we are assailed with data constantly and need to make decisions quickly.

The rise of AI and deepfakes has accelerated exponentially in 2024, to the extent that it has been deemed as one of the world's "biggest short-term threats."[4] In this context, journalists' role as verifiers has gained paramount importance. But the 'democratization' of media, and the reduced gatekeeping role of traditional media, means fact-checking, verification and media literacy also need to be part of the broader skillset of digital citizens.

Check your facts

Fact-checking initiatives in the Global South have been pioneering innovative, AI-powered approaches to combat misinformation and reach diverse audiences. In Brazil, Aos Fatos's AI-powered bot, Fátima, operates across various social media platforms, allowing users to easily access their database of fact-checks. Additionally, Aos Fatos developed an algorithm called Radar, which monitors language patterns potentially linked to misinformation across different platforms.[5]

Africa has also seen significant growth in fact-checking initiatives, with Africa Check at the forefront. Launched in 2012, Africa Check has fostered a network of 20 member organizations across the continent, with innovative programs combining in-person workshops, online tutorials and multi-platform content.[6] It is also exploring the use of radio dramas to disseminate fact-checked information to communities without reliable internet connectivity.

1   Rawnsley, A. (2020, July 6) 'Right-Wing Media Outlets Duped by a Middle East Propaganda Campaign', The Daily Beast. Retrieved from: thedailybeast.com/right-wing-media-outlets-duped-by-a-middle-east-propaganda-campaign

2   Kovach, B. & Rosenstiel, T. (2001, June 15) 'The Essence of Journalism is a Discipline of Verification', Nieman Reports. Retrieved from: niemanreports.org/articles/the-essence-of-journalism-is-a-discipline-of-verification/

3   Kavanagh, J. and Rich, M. D. (2018, January 16) 'Truth Decay: An Initial Exploration of the Diminishing Role of Facts and Analysis in American Public Life'. Santa Monica, California: RAND Corporation.

4   Elliott, L. (2024, January 10) 'AI-Driven Misinformation "Biggest Short-Term Threat to Global Economy"', The Guardian. Retrieved from: theguardian.com/business/2024/jan/10/ai-driven-misinformation-biggest-short-term-threat-to-global-economy

5   Tameez, H. (2024, January 9) 'This Brazilian fact-checking org uses a ChatGPT-esque bot to answer reader questions', NiemanLab. Retrieved from: niemanlab.org/2024/01/this-brazilian-fact-checking-org-uses-a-chatgpt-esque-bot-to-answer-reader-questions/

6   Tillmann, P. (2020, May 20) 'Media Start-Up: Africa Check in South Africa', Deutsche Welle. Retrieved from: akademie.dw.com/en/media-start-up-africa-check-in-south-africa/a-53517750

7   'About Boom: An IFCN Certified Fact Checker' (2018) BOOM. Retrieved from: boomlive.in/about-us

In India, BOOM has adapted its fact-checking services to the country's linguistic diversity. Operating in Hindi, English and Bengali, BOOM also maintains local websites for Myanmar and Bangladesh. [7] Its WhatsApp helpline allows individuals to submit information for verification and its work debunking fake news during the Israel-Gaza war was pivotal due to the large amount of disinformation emanating from pro-Modi social media accounts. [8]

Beyond the Global South, organizations like Bellingcat, an open-source intelligence group, has gained recognition for its thorough verification work, notably in identifying Russian military personnel involved in the shooting down of the MH17. [9]

The challenges of verification

Journalists often find themselves caught between the pressure to break news quickly and the need for thorough fact-checking. The rise of deepfakes and AI-generated content has further complicated this task, making it increasingly difficult to distinguish authentic material from sophisticated fabrications. The rapid spread of information on social media platforms can outpace the verification process, allowing false narratives to gain traction before they can be debunked. Even then, many people who consumed the false content will rarely read the correction or fact-checked version.

Monetary incentives are also muddying the waters of reality. Elon Musk's decision to abandon identity-based verification on X (see page 42 for more) is an example of this. Now people can pay a subscription fee to have their content boosted, without documents proving they are even who they claim to be. In short, bad actors can pay for propaganda, just because social media companies are prioritizing profit. [10]

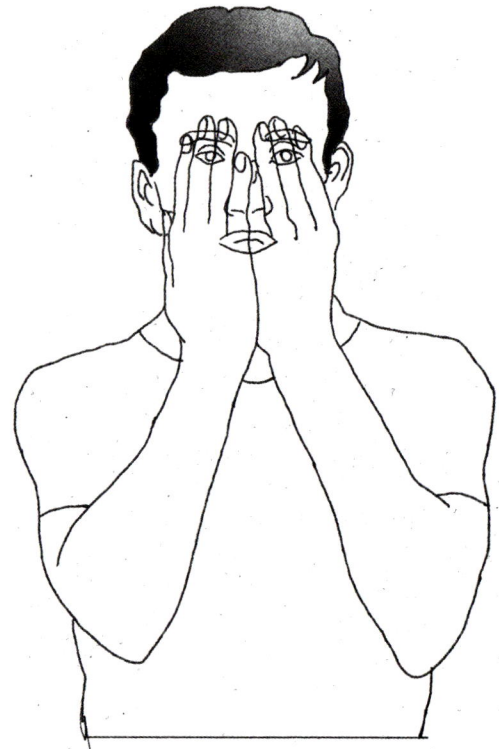

In an age of AI and automation, determining what is real, and what is human, is increasingly difficult. The importance of verification needs to be instilled not just in journalists, but in all those who care about the truth. Without verification, there is only speculation.

8 Chowdhury, A. (2023, October 11) 'Verified X Indian Accounts Spread Disinformation on Israel-Hamas Conflict', BOOM. Retrieved from: boomlive.in/news/israel-palestine-gaza-hamas-middle-east-war-conflict-fake-news-disinfo-meghupdates-ajaychauhan41-mrsinha-jix5a-twitter-x-23311

9 Van Huis, P. et al, 'Identifying the Separatists Linked to the Downing of MH17' (2019, June 19), Bellingcat. Retrieved from: bellingcat.com/news/uk-and-europe/2019/06/19/identifying-the-separatists-linked-to-the-downing-of-mh17/

10 Hammond-Errey, M. (2023, July 15) 'Elon Musk's Twitter Is Becoming a Sewer of Disinformation', Foreign Policy. Retrieved from: foreignpolicy.com/2023/07/15/elon-musk-twitter-blue-checks-verification-disinformation-propaganda-russia-china-trust-safety/

Related terms

→   Truth decay
→   Post-truth
→   Deepfakes
→   Gatekeeping
→   Open-source intelligence
→   Citizen journalism
→   AI-powered bot
→   Digital citizens
→   Media literacy
→   Disinformation
→   Misinformation

Further reading

Kovach, B., & Rosenstiel, T. (2014) The Elements of Journalism: What Newspeople Should Know and the Public Should Expect. New York: Three Rivers Press.

Verification Handbook: A Definitive Guide to Verifying Digital Content for Emergency Coverage (2014) Silverman, C. ed. Maastricht: European Journalism Centre.

Wardle, C., & Derakhshan, H. (2017) Information Disorder: Toward an interdisciplinary framework for research and policy making. Strasbourg Cedex: Council of Europe.

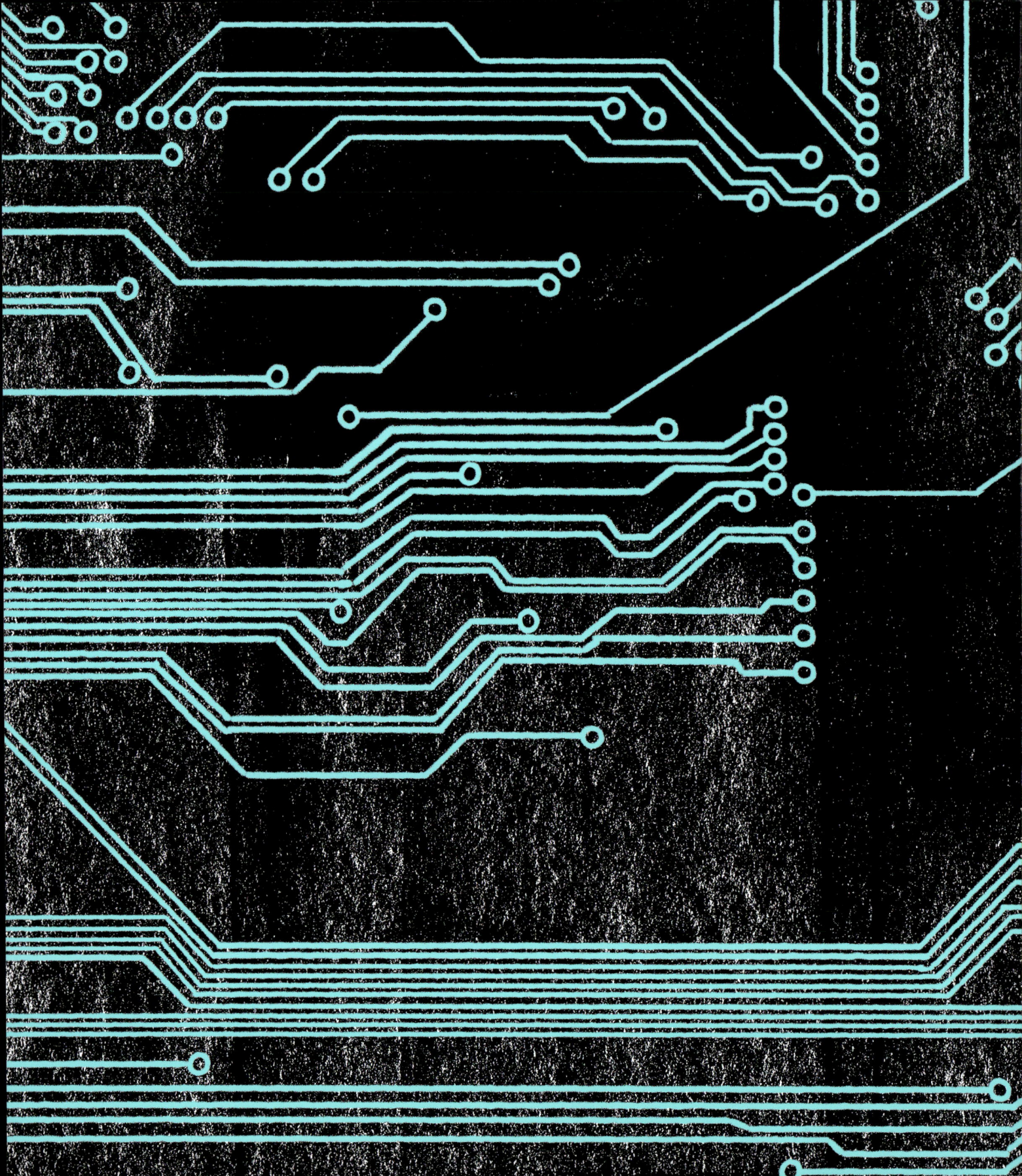

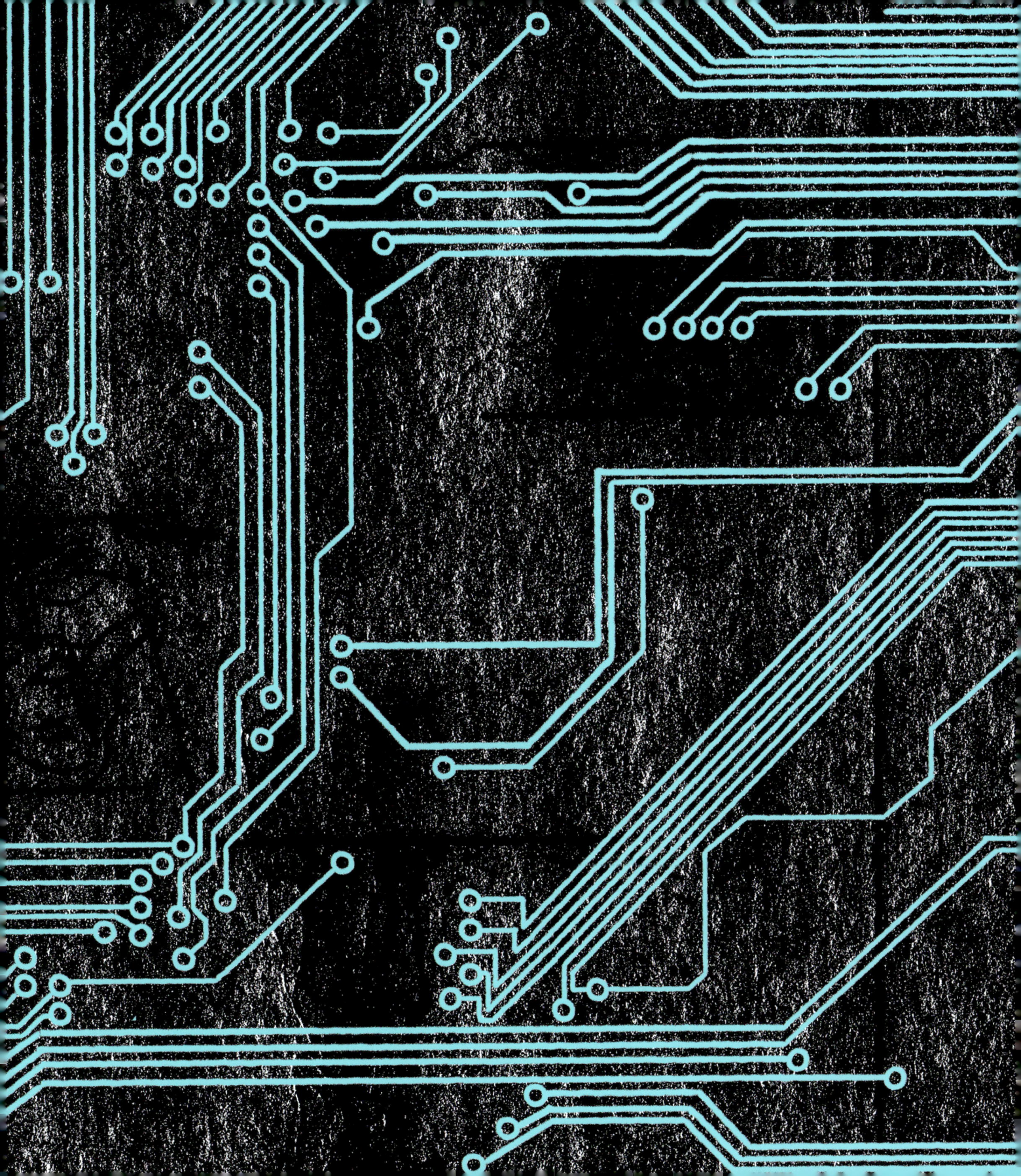

Endword: On decision-making processes in the age of AI

By Alfredo Cramerotti

There is a peculiar sensation in the air—one of inevitability, perhaps, or something more elusive: the sense that we are being drawn, inexorably, into a future that is already half-written by the algorithms that increasingly govern our lives. It's a sensation that seeps into the crevices of our daily routines, into the choices we make without a second thought and even into the decisions we agonize over. AI, once the stuff of science fiction, is now embedded in the very fabric of our existence, shaping how we think, how we create, how we govern. And in this new socio-cultural-scientific landscape, the question that lingers and refuses to be dismissed is not merely how AI influences our decision-making processes, but what it means for the future of human agency itself.

In my curatorial practice and broader engagement with the art and media worlds, I often stand at the intersection of technology and creativity, where the promise of AI is met with both excitement and trepidation. AI, with its unmatched ability to process data and recognize patterns, is often hailed as the key to unlocking new frontiers of decision-making and efficiency in practically every field. It can sort through vast amounts of information in seconds, predict trends with uncanny accuracy and even suggest decisions that might never have occurred to a human mind. But as I consider the implications of this technological prowess, I wonder—not with fear, but with a kind of cautious curiosity—what becomes of the uniquely human elements of judgment and intuition and empathy in this new age? Take, for instance, the world of healthcare. IBM's Watson data analytics processor, or platforms devised using TensorFlow open-source machine learning framework (written about in this volume by Katy Gillett), are good examples of AI in action. Watson, despite some setbacks and 'overpromising and underdelivering,' has partially transformed the way medical professionals diagnose and treat patients over the last two decades. It can cross-reference millions of data points, pulling from vast medical

libraries to offer treatment recommendations that are, in many cases, more precise than those of any single doctor. It has evolved and is deployed for many other business use cases—including customer service, supply chain, financial planning, risk and compliance, advertising, IT, video and security at scale. Taken as a whole 'ecosystem,' the efficiencies of such a system are undeniable, and yet, one must ask: what is lost in the translation of human experience into data? Is there a way to integrate the irreplaceable art of medical judgment—the instinct honed by years of patient care—with the computational power of AI? The future may lay not in AI replacing human judgment, but in augmenting it, creating a symbiosis where the strengths of both are fully realized. That's the overarching goal.

In the realm of criminal justice, for instance, where the stakes are often life and liberty, AI-driven tools like COMPAS (Correctional Offender Management Profiling for Alternative Sanctions)—a management and decision support tool developed and owned by a private company and used by courts in the USA to assess the likelihood of a defendant becoming a recidivist—have been introduced to guide sentencing decisions. On paper, these tools offer a promise of objectivity, a way to eliminate the biases that have long plagued the justice system. But reality complicates the narrative. The data used to train these algorithms is pretty much a reflection of historical injustices, and thus, the AI systems often perpetuate the very biases they are meant to eliminate—a warning that several of the authors in this book have repeatedly stated for different causes.

A call to engage more deeply with the ethical frameworks that govern our use of technology is highly due. If we are to rely on AI in such critical decisions, then we must also be vigilant in ensuring that the algorithms are transparent, that they are subject to scrutiny, that they are designed with an acute awareness of the social contexts in which they operate, and that there is accountability implemented for when they fail. All still far away from actuality. Currently, it is in the creative industries—my own world—where the potential for AI to reshape decision-making is both most exciting and most fraught.

Generative Adversarial Networks (GANs) are now capable of producing art that challenges our very notions of creativity and authorship. As a curator, often working with artists very active in the digital realm, I have witnessed how AI can help produce outstanding works (often based on custom-made databases by the artists themselves), analyze audience preferences, predict and interpret trends, maximize marketing actions and even suggest (heaven forbid) artworks that align with a particular theme or concept. On one hand, this can lead to more engaging, more focused and more personalized exhibitions. On the other, I understand the process of curation in exhibitions—the delicate, intuitive act of selection and contextualization, of juxtaposition and suggestion—could become overly deterministic, guided more by data than by the curator's vision. Yet rather than resisting this shift, I am intrigued by the possibilities. Could AI not serve as a collaborator, a critical friend, a tool that expands the curator's horizon rather than narrows it? The challenge, I believe, lies in striking a meaningful (not necessarily productive) balance—using AI to enhance the creative process without allowing it to dominate. How to get that balance right, remains to be seen—and crucially, experienced.

As entire industries and society's sectors, as well as governments around the world, begin to incorporate AI into their operation and administration—from optimizing traffic systems to deploying predictive policing—the conversation must keep shifting from a focus on efficiency to a broader discussion about the values we wish to embed in our technological systems. I do not think we talk enough—or at least publicly enough—about these values. Efficiency, after all, is not the only measure of success. Equity, justice, well-being, a sense of things being well thought-out and made (I am a curator, after all, and I value aesthetics), and the preservation of human dignity are, for me, equally

important. The future of AI is not about replacing human decision-makers, but about equipping them with tools that can help them make better, more informed and more equitable decisions—tools that are transparent, accountable and aligned with the principles of society. In reflecting on these developments, I return to a central thought: AI's greatest potential lies not in its ability to transcend human limitations, but in its capacity to work alongside us, enhancing our decision-making processes while leaving room for the human elements of empathy, intuition, moral judgment and even beauty. Or, as Ali Al Kubaisi mentions in 'Z is for Zero,': "This binary approach can be problematic because it oversimplifies the complexity of human sentiment." Indeed.

We must not view AI as a panacea, nor as a threat, but as a partner—a collaborator in the ongoing project of human progress. And a companion in the long journey of human culture. The real challenge, as we move forward, is to ensure that our use of AI is guided by a thoughtful consideration of its implications. We must ask ourselves not only what AI can do, but what it should do. The decisions we make about AI today will shape the future of decision-making itself, determining whether technology serves as a tool for human empowerment, or whether we become subservient to the very systems we create. The future is not yet written, and it is within our power to guide its course. In the end, the question is not whether AI will change the way we make decisions—this much is inevitable. The question is how we will navigate this change, ensuring that in our pursuit of innovation, we do not lose sight of the deeper, more human aspects of decision-making; because the most important decisions are not those made by AI, but those made about AI. The answers will not come easily, nor should they. But in asking the right questions—in engaging critically and creatively with the possibilities of AI—we may yet find a way to harness its potential in ways that enrich, rather than diminish, the human experience.

Biographies

Contributors

Mohammad Shayan Ahmad

A sophomore from Pakistan, Mohammad Shayan Ahmad is studying at Northwestern University in Qatar, majoring in Communications and Media Industries, while minoring in Film and Design. Ahmad aspires to be a data visualizer, focusing on 3D display and visualizations. For this publication, he focuses on X, formerly known as Twitter, a social media platform that has been highly popularized throughout his formative years. Outside of his academic interests, he also loves reading about new scientific discoveries, especially in cosmology.

Ali Al Kubaisi

With a Bachelor's degree in Chemical Engineering and a Master's degree in Engineering Management, Ali Al Kubaisi is driven by the opportunity to be part of the narrative that shapes new technologies and integrates them into our cultures. He is passionate about how technology is shaping the future of industries, with a robust curiosity for innovation. His research background in digital transformation focuses on identifying key factors that enable industries to adopt and thrive with new technologies.

Hannah Al Mannai

Qatari student Hannah Al Mannai is a Journalism Junior at Northwestern University in Qatar, a subject she's pursuing thanks to a long passion for and interest in stories about politics. So far, Al Mannai has taken several courses on political science, history and journalistic writing, which have pushed her to discover a world beyond her own perspective. She strives to take this experience into her role as a research assistant at the Media Majlis Museum.

Hind Al Saad

The work of Qatari graphic designer and computational artist Hind Al Saad folds Islamic and cultural principles into the medium of computation and print. She was the fifth artist-in-residence at the Fire Station in Doha and is part of The Ned Doha art collection. She holds an MFA in Design from VCUArts Qatar and taught at the School for Poetic Computation. She collaborates with xLab, a studio for new making and computation, where she co-curated and co-produced the Language-as-Machine exhibition.

Rashid Al-Mohanadi

With experience in the LNG and defence industry, Rashid Al-Mohanadi has supported founding many functions within the ecosystem, including R&D and system development. He currently holds a senior position within business development. He also runs his consultancy focusing on insurance, anti-economic crime, security and anti-illicit trade advisory services. He holds a Bachelor of Engineering from the University of Surrey, a Master's in Critical Security Studies from the Doha Institute, and a Master's in Defense and Security Studies from the Joaan Military Academy.

Salim Al-Shuaili

Omani award-winning professional Salim Al-Shuaili works in the realm of Information Technology and Artificial Intelligence, with a career spanning 22 years and various sectors, including mining, smart cities, healthcare, education and media. He has a Ph.D. in ICT, specializing in technology adoption, AI and digital transformation. He currently serves as the Director of the Artificial Intelligence and Advanced Technology Projects Unit, and is also the founder and CEO of MasaraTech, which specializes in consultation, development and training in the technology field.

Mohammed Al-Sulaiti

Mohammed Al-Sulaiti recently earned his Ph.D. from the Centre for Environmental Policy at Imperial College London. His thesis examined environmental and climate change legislation in Qatar, particularly focusing on the impact of big data science and its associated emissions. During his studies, Al-Sulaiti worked with cloud entities to help design sustainability strategies, aiming to reduce their environmental footprint. He is dedicated to understanding and improving environmental policies, hoping his research can contribute to Qatar's efforts in addressing climate change.

Jasmina Bondare

Jasmina Bondare is a Journalism Junior at Northwestern University in Qatar, dedicated to giving a voice to minorities and women through writing and film. Her experience as the Vice President of Studio 20Q, as an intern at Qatar Museums' Public Art curation department and Latvia's TV24, have developed her storytelling skills. Bondare intends to pursue a Master's in Human Rights and Global Justice, aiming to advocate for marginalized communities through her future work.

Eddy Borges-Rey

Digital journalism and emerging media are the subjects to which Eddy Borges-Rey has dedicated his career. With extensive academic expertise in these areas, he is now an Associate Professor at Northwestern University in Qatar. He is the co-editor of the book series Palgrave Studies in Journalism and the Global South, and, prior to obtaining a Master's and Ph.D. in Media and Communication, Borges-Rey worked as a broadcast journalist, media producer and PR practitioner for almost 15 years.

David Caswell

David Caswell is the founder of StoryFlow Ltd, an innovation consultancy focused on AI in journalism. He was previously the Executive Product Manager of BBC News Labs and has held senior roles leading AI initiatives at Yahoo!, Tribune Publishing and The Los Angeles Times. Caswell also publishes peer-reviewed research on computational and automated forms of journalism. He is a frequent speaker and writer about the opportunities and challenges facing journalism in the emerging AI-mediated digital media ecosystem.

Alfredo Cramerotti

A cultural entrepreneur working at the intersection of contemporary art, media and technology, Alfredo Cramerotti is currently the director of the Media Majlis Museum at Northwestern Qatar. He is president of IKT–International Association Curators of Contemporary Art, chair of the Digital Strategies Committee of AICA–International Association of Art Critics, and advisor to the KSA Visual Art Commission, UK Government Art Collection, British Council Visual Arts Acquisition Committee and the Italian Ministry of Culture. Cramerotti has also written over 200 published texts on contemporary art and media theory.

Sashreek Garg

A student at Northwestern University in Qatar, Sashreek Garg is pursuing a degree in Journalism, Media, and Integrated Marketing Communications, as well as minors in Strategic Communications and Media & Politics. He is passionate about research, documentary filmmaking, marketing and public relations, and has held internships with international and regional media organizations, including Fox Sports, FIFA, Grey Group, Grayling and Zee Media. He was also a Global Undergraduate Fellow at the Institute for Advanced Study in the Global South.

Katy Gillett

With a career spanning almost two decades, Katy Gillett is currently a freelance journalist and editor based in Dubai. She was previously the Head of Arts & Lifestyle at The National and has contributed to a wide range of publications and media outlets including Time Out, British GQ, Conde Nast Traveller, The Unesco Courier, Euronews and British Vogue. She regularly works with the Museum Majlis Museum at Northwestern University in Qatar developing and editing publications for the museum's exhibitions.

Marwan M. Kraidy

Marwan M. Kraidy is Dean and CEO of Northwestern University in Qatar. Kraidy is also a Professor of Communication and the Anthony Shadid Chair in Global Media, Politics and Culture at Northwestern. In 2021, Kraidy founded the Institute for Advanced Study in the Global South, which is dedicated to evidence-based storytelling on the diverse histories, cultures, societies and media of the Global South. Kraidy has also authored 13 award-winning books and more than 130 articles, essays and chapters, and is the winner of over 50 awards for teaching and scholarship.

Maria Lisboa-Ward

Originally from southern Brazil, Maria Lisboa-Ward is a rising senior studying Journalism and Strategic Communications at Northwestern University in Qatar and a Research Fellow at the Institute for Advanced Study in the Global South, where her research focuses on class and authenticity in Brazilian social media. She moved abroad for the first time at 16 years old, and has since studied and worked in the USA, UK, Middle East and Europe.

Iqra Mazhar Hussain

As a senior majoring in Journalism at Northwestern University in Qatar, Iqra Mazhar Hussain has had the opportunity to write on topics related to women's rights, fashion, tourism and other social issues. She has also gained valuable experience in news writing and editing while completing an internship at a news broadcasting channel and hopes to continue creating impactful stories. In her free time, she also likes to read, travel and watch Turkish TV shows.

Syed Mehdi

Currently, Syed Mehdi is the Manager of Technology and Operations at the Media Majlis Museum at Northwestern University in Qatar, and previously worked for FIFA World Cup Qatar 2022™ as an analyst leading the development of applications and dashboards for procurement and operations. He has also worked as a researcher for Carnegie Mellon University Qatar, developing natural language processing tools for the Arabic language. He holds a Bachelor of Science in Information Systems from Carnegie Mellon University.

Cheng Mei

Technology news that impacts daily life is what Cheng Mei (Anthony) focuses on in his work, with a lens on China and other Global South regions. He provides in-depth analysis of the relationship between humanity and technology, and he is passionate about inspiring his fellow reporters to keep the human element at the forefront of their storytelling. He is currently a senior at Northwestern University in Qatar, majoring in Journalism.

Marc Owen Jones

As an Associate Professor of Media Analytics at Northwestern University in Qatar, Marc Owen Jones lectures and researches on disinformation, digital authoritarianism and political repression. Among his various publications are Political Repression in Bahrain and Disinformation and Deception in the Middle East. Jones regularly appears on channels such as BBC and CBC, and has written for international media outlets, including The Washington Post, CNN, Time magazine, The Independent and the New Statesman, and has a regular column on Al Jazeera English.

Maryam Rashid Al-Khater

Award-winning media professional Maryam Rashid Al-Khater is Professor of Media and Digital Communications, and Advisor to the President of Qatar University. Her fields of expertise include media, social media, and political and social movements, and she holds a Ph.D. in Political Communications. She is the Vice Chair of the Media Committee for the Preparation of Media and Journalism Terminologies Dictionary in Arabic. She has published several research papers and books in media and been appointed to various media boards and committees.

Farjana Salahuddin

As an interactive and new media artist, Farjana Salahuddin intends to create a bridge between the traditional and digital by blending tangible work with the power of computing and real-time dynamic audiovisual arts through collaborations with artists from various disciplines. Her work has spanned a range of themes and mediums, with showcases in Washington D.C. and Qatar. Salahuddin holds a Master's in Interactive Digital Media from Trinity College Dublin, and a Bachelor's in Information Systems from Carnegie Mellon University.

Jack Thomas Taylor

Jack Thomas Taylor is the Curator of Art, Media and Technology at the Media Majlis Museum. He holds an MA and MBA from Central Saint Martins and is currently a Ph.D. researcher at King's College London. With extensive experience in curating, cultural strategy and publishing across the Arabian Peninsula, Taylor has spearheaded numerous exhibitions exploring contemporary media and cultural themes. Taylor is a founding board member of ICOM Qatar.

Wajdi Zaghouani

Wajdi Zaghouani is an Associate Professor in Residence in Communication at Northwestern University in Qatar. He holds a Ph.D. in Natural Language Processing and his research in computational linguistics spans Arabic data analytics, linguistic annotation, fake news detection and sentiment analysis. He has secured over $6 million in research grants from QNRF, supporting projects such as the MARSAD Social Media observatory and hate speech detection in Arabic social media. Zaghouani has also consulted for big data companies and organized numerous international conferences.

Amal Zeyad Ali

With extensive experience as a museum curator and cultural producer based in Qatar, Amal Zeyad Ali is currently the Assistant Curator at the Media Majlis Museum, at Northwestern University in Qatar, and was previously the Programs Associate. She has also served as an Exhibitions Coordinator at the Artist in Residence program at the Fire Station in Doha. She is a graduate of Northwestern University in Qatar, class of 2018.

Credits

Artists and lenders

Adnan Ayub Aga
Amr Alngmah
Barjeel Art Foundation, Sharjah, UAE
Bilge Emir
Christto Andrew
Computer History Museum,
        California, USA
Dartmouth College,
        New Hampshire, USA
Dries Depoorter
Entangled Others, Lisbon, Portugal
Farjana Salahuddin
Feileacan K. McCormick
Galerie Hors-Cadre, Paris, France
Getty Images
Hadeer Omar
Hind Al Saad
Jan Zuiderveld
Joey Holder
Kate Crawford
Mathieu Merlet Briand
Museum of Fine Arts, Boston, USA
Patrick Tresset
Qatar Museums
Raqs Media Collective,
        New Delhi, India
Rashid Al Sulaiti
Scala Archives, Florence, Italy
Shutterstock
Sofia Crespo
Vladan Joler
Warana, Amsterdam,
        The Netherlands

Exhibition team

Ai or Nay? Artificial vs. Intelligent
Media Majlis Museum
Northwestern Qatar
15 January – 15 May, 2025

Curator
Jack Thomas Taylor

Researcher
Ali Al Kubaisi

Creative advisory
Hind Al Saad, Hadeer Omar
Farjana Salahuddin

Scenography
Khaled Alawadhi and
Rawan Alkhuzai of fortytwelve,
Kuwait

Creative direction
Andreas Märki, Nils Braun,
Pamina Gisler, and Reham Mohamed
of Studio Flux, Switzerland

Digital content
Bram Bogaerts, Robin Smits, Casper
Schipper and Sjoerd Mol of Superposition, The Netherlands

Copy editing
Katy Gillett

Interpretation
Claire Dobbin

Student researchers
Mohammad Shayan Ahmad,
Hannah Al Mannai, Jasmina Bondare,
Sashreek Garg, Maria Lisboa-Ward,
Iqra Mazhar Hussain, Cheng Mei

Arabic proofreading
Salam Shughry and Hanna Majed

Museum team

Media Majlis Museum

Director
Alfredo Cramerotti

Curator of Art, Media and Technology
Jack Thomas Taylor

Assistant Curator
Amal Ali

Collection Development
and Care Manager
Hicham Al-Baker

Manager of Integrated Marketing
& Digital Content
Shahnawaz Zali

Manager of Technology
and Operations
Syed Mehdi

Manager of Audience
and Community Outreach
Safa Arshad

Audience and Front of
House Associate
Maha Nasr

Contractors

GWC Logistics, Fine Art Shipment and Installation; Interspace Qatar, Build and Construction; Qatar Translation Center, Translation, Bespoke, Spatial Layout; Astucemedia, Digital User Interface Design; Flint Culture, PR and Communications; Gulfcrafts Co, Branding and Wayfinding; Maktaba Children's Library, Educational Programming; Artworks Conservation, Facsimile and Replicas; Laurent Jakimow Web Solutions, Digital Labels; Morris Hargreaves McIntyre, Audience Insight & Evaluation.

Imprint

Preferred citation: when referencing this edited volume in its entirety, please use the following citation:

Taylor, J. T. & Gillett, K. eds. (2025) A Glossary: Artificial vs. Intelligent. Italy: Silvana Editoriale.

When referencing specific contributions, please use the following format:

Surname, Initial(s). (2025) ['Title of Contribution'], A Glossary: Artificial vs. Intelligent, Taylor, J. T. & Gillett, K., eds. Italy: Silvana Editoriale. [Page Number(s) XX–XX].

Silvana Editoriale

General Director
Michele Pizzi

Editorial Director
Sergio Di Stefano

Art Director
Giacomo Merli

Editorial Coordinator
Maria Chiara Tulli

Graphic Design
Federico Zavatta – Contrast Design

Copy Editing
Filomena Moscatelli

Production Coordinator
Antonio Micelli

Editorial Assistant
Giulia Mercanti

Iconographic Office
Silvia Sala

Press Office
Alessandra Olivari, press@silvanaeditoriale.it

ISBN 9788836655472

MISTO
Carta | A sostegno della
gestione forestale responsabile
FSC® C116320
FSC
www.fsc.org

Available through ARTBOOK | D.A.P.
155 Sixth Avenue, 2nd Floor,
New York, N.Y. 10013
Tel: (212) 627-1999
Fax: (212) 627-9484

Silvana Editoriale S.p.A.
via dei Lavoratori, 78
20092 Cinisello Balsamo, Milano
tel. 02 453 951 01
www.silvanaeditoriale.it

Reproductions, printing and binding in Italy
Printed by Grafiche Lang S.r.l., Genova
in December 2024